Jane Rubietta's [writing is so powerful] that it captivate[s the reader. She has a] new and fresh [way ... unusual] way of expressing new ironies in these age-old stories of the Bible. I love that! Through these devotionals, you'll be reading a familiar story again, but seeing it as if for the first time. You're going to love this book. I do!

—DIANNE E. BUTTS, author of six books, including *Deliver Me*

Jane Rubietta brings a sensitivity to her writing that establishes an immediate bond between Jane and her readers. Her insights are wise, her lessons are practical, and her message is encouraging. Read and be refreshed!

—DENNIS E. HENSLEY, author of *Jesus in the 9 to 5*

Finding Your Promise is a lovely journey to the miraculous lives found in the Bible. This is a devotional that is also a study in discipleship, yet it carries readers from barren to bounty, telling the story of Abraham in a beautiful, exquisite manner. More than a deeply personal Bible study in devotion, this is also a perfect discipleship tool for small groups.

—KATHI MACIAS, award-winning author of more than forty books, including *The Singing Quilt*

In *Finding Your Promise*, Jane Rubietta leads us on the captivating journey of the life of Abraham. Her writing is powerful, visual, and impactful. Jane is a gifted wordsmith who captures the essence of developing an intimate connection with God while challenging the reader to do the same. This book is filled with practical applications and opportunities for personal reflection. Don't miss it!

—CAROL KENT, speaker, best-selling author of *When I Lay My Isaac Down* and *Unquenchable*

These are transformational devotionals with great depth. Jane offers a fresh and compelling vision of the life of Abraham, but more than rich words, she has coupled biblical truth with practical ways in which to personally walk from barren to bounty. Especially transformational can be her guide, which leads one to read, contemplate, and act. There is rich and practical depth in these pages.

—JO ANNE LYON, General Superintendent, The Wesleyan Church

Jane Rubietta invites us on a journey from barren to bounty through the life of Abraham that will surprise and inspire you. Packed with Scripture and written with personal witness and wisdom, this ninety-two-day adventure calls us to not only understand, but also live in the promise of full, new life.

—ANDREA SUMMERS, Director of Ministry for Women; The Wesleyan Church

With real-life stories and engaging insight from the Bible, Jane leads readers from barren to bounty to make the life of Abraham real in our lives. What a brilliant connection! Let Jane lead you there—and gain fresh faith and hope for your journey.

—THADDEUS BARNUM, author of *Real Identity* and *Real Love*; senior pastor of Church of the Apostles, Fairfield, Connecticut

FINDING YOUR
Promise

FINDING YOUR
Promise

FROM BARREN TO BOUNTY—
THE LIFE OF ABRAHAM

Jane Rubietta

wphstore.com

Copyright © 2015 by Jane Rubietta
Published by Wesleyan Publishing House
Indianapolis, Indiana 46250
Printed in the United States of America
ISBN: 978-0-89827-896-5
ISBN (e-book): 978-0-89827-897-2

Library of Congress Cataloging-in-Publication Data

Rubietta, Jane.
　Finding your promise : from barren to bounty--the life of Abraham / Jane Rubietta.
　　pages cm
　ISBN 978-0-89827-896-5 (pbk.)
1. Bible. Genesis, XII-XXV--Devotional literature. 2. Abraham (Biblical patriarch)--Meditations. I. Title.
　BS1235.54.R83 2014
　222'.1106--dc23
　　　　　　　　　　　　　　　2014020196

All Scripture quotations, unless otherwise indicated, are taken from the Holy Bible, New International Version®, NIV ®. Copyright ©1973, 1978, 1984, 2011 by Biblica, Inc. Used by permission of Zondervan. All rights reserved worldwide. www.zondervan.com. The "NIV" and "New International Version" are trademarks registered in the United States Patent and Trademark Office by Biblica, Inc.

Scripture quotations marked (NIV84) are taken from the Holy Bible, New International Version®, NIV ®. Copyright © 1973, 1978, 1984 by Biblica, Inc. Used by permission of Zondervan. All rights reserved worldwide. www.zondervan.com. The "NIV" and "New International Version" are trademarks registered in the United States Patent and Trademark Office by Biblica, Inc.

Scripture quotations marked (MSG) are taken from *The Message*. Copyright © 1993, 1994, 1995, 1996, 2000, 2001, 2002. Used by permission of NavPress Publishing Group.

Scripture quotations marked (NET) are from the NET Bible® copyright ©1996–2006 by Biblical Studies Press, L.L.C. http://bible.org. All rights reserved. Used by permission.

Cover photo: Cody Rayn

All rights reserved. No part of this publication may be reproduced, stored in a retrieval system, or transmitted in any form or by any means—electronic, mechanical, photocopy, recording, or any other—except for brief quotations in printed reviews, without the prior written permission of the publisher.

To our gracious God who delights to fulfill all those promises.
And to all who wait for their fulfillment.

"The Lord is trustworthy in all he promises
and faithful in all he does."
—Psalm 145:13

CONTENTS

Introduction	11
March Devotions	13
April Devotions	113
May Devotions	211
About the Author	313

For a free group leader's guide,
visit www.wphresources.com/findingyourpromise.

INTRODUCTION

Desert travel is not for the faint of heart. When flying from Chicago's O'Hare airport to the West Coast, I marvel at the rugged terrain between Lake Michigan and the Pacific Ocean. Mountains and plains and deserts and great caverns. Even more, I marvel at the rugged people who trekked from the East Coast clear across the country to settle out west.

I'm not sure how far I would have lasted on the journey, even if I had known what awaited me. So many people caravanned west, full of optimism and a spirit of adventure. How long en route before they succumbed to despondency or illness? How many people turned back? At what point did they decide that it's either go forward or die trying?

As we explore the life of Abraham, one of our most famous ancestors of the faith, and the lives of his family members, we will journey with them from Ur, where God first called Abraham, to Canaan, then to Egypt, and back to Canaan again, until his son Isaac took over the family dynasty. Though difficult to date with precision, their journey occurred sometime in the

Middle Bronze II era, around 2200–1600 BC. The complicated lives and choices of these forbearers of the faith grant us plenty of room to relate, to empathize, and to see ourselves reflected in their choices and situations.

Even more than that, we trace the faithfulness of the God who called Abraham then, and who calls us today. Calls us into a life of promise, of possibility. Calls us from our barren lives into lives laden with bounty.

That's a promise.

Finding Your Promise is an inspiring, hopeful guide for all who long for a deeper devotion, for more in their relationship with God and others. For all who long to break free from the snares of today and the prisons of yesterday. For all who hope for new insights into old truths; for new skin on familiar, sometimes worn-out stories; for new life in their old life.

In over ninety warm, challenging deeper devotions, each with an opening Scripture, a daily reading, a "Traveling Mercy" benediction, and a one-sentence "Note to Self," *Finding Your Promise* is an invitation from God to come, gather perspective, and be refreshed, rehydrated, and ready to journey on. Our walk through Genesis 12–25 will offer fresh eyes to see Abraham, Sarah, their contemporaries, and their descendants; fresh application to turn from them toward our own souls; and fresh understandings for our own journeys. *Finding Your Promise* will do more than open the Scriptures. It will change the way we experience our travels and our God.

Finding Your Promise. A travel guide for pilgrims, leading to the Promised Land, and to the One who promised.

MARCH DEVOTIONS

MARCH 1

INTERRUPTING THE EVERYDAY

The LORD had said to Abram, "Go from your country,
your people and your father's household."

—GENESIS 12:1

Abraham's adventure begins like our own stories. Most of us live an everyday, normal, very average existence. We experience disappointment, grief, laughter, love, surprise, and loss. We get up each day and plug along, minding our own business, perhaps excessively, and then, in the middle of our tepid tedium, our world shifts. God speaks into the long run-on sentence of our life. Just so, God interrupted the everydayness of Abraham's life with a simple command: "Go."

Abraham, then known as Abram, had never heard from this God. We have no record of his family carrying a gilt-edged family Bible from Ur, no ledger of family offerings or prayers. Nothing.

Whether on a whim or to escape the place where Abram's father, Terah, buried one of his sons or in response to a subtle unspoken call from God, Terah and his entire family schlepped hundreds of miles from Ur to Harran. They abandoned Babylon's thriving culture—left behind the commerce, nightlife, pagan festivals; forfeited jobs and social standing; ditched their friends.

When Terah up and died,[1] God planted a bug in Abram's ear: Go. Do all that again.

Seriously? God just said, "You've never heard of me; no one sang you lullabies about me. No 'Kum Bah Yah' around the campfire. But here's the deal: Leave everything—your country, relatives, father's household, the life you've been living. Everything that you base your identity upon."

If Abram had the least track record of God's calling or provision, going might have made sense. If Abram had seen God's faithfulness, noting it in his journal, he could have nodded and said, "OK. This worked before. I'll take this calculated risk based on what I already know."

Except he didn't *already* know anything about this God. Start your engines, because here comes the miracle.

An amazing feature of the finding and calling of Abram is that *God* found and called. Maybe it is *the* amazing feature of the storyboard of this man's life. But it reveals something bigger than one man's life, this man who lived four thousand years ago. This is part of the miracle, because it is about us too.

The very God of the universe, the God who created heaven and earth, the God who broke apart the endless night with light and hung the stars in the sky, the moon for a nightlight, and the sun to brighten the day—this God enters into our daily lives, the very dailyness of our ordinary lives, and speaks to us.

But he not only speaks. That would be incredible and unbelievable enough.

He makes promises to us. Promises! It's almost laughable, it's so unbelievable and so undeserved and so unnecessary. Did God *need* to reach out to us?

The great God of heaven, the one true God, the Creator of the universe, comes to us and makes promises to us, calling us from our insignificance and anonymity into relationship, into covenant, into meaning, into purpose.

It's almost unbelievable, yes, except that it's the puzzle piece that fits perfectly into the hole in our soul, that deep crevasse of endless emptiness. It answers fully and completely an unutterable ache we experience, or mostly try to avoid or satisfy with substitutes—a longing for relationship, for meaning, for something bigger than our day-to-day plodding steps that go nowhere but in circles of insignificance.

This sense of futility and obscurity groans within us all.

And so God's voice penetrates into the finiteness of our walled-in existence and finds a custom-made and waiting home in us.

This is one miracle of Genesis, the book of beginnings, the story of the beginning of a call and a promise unlike any we could imagine. The miracle of beginning with God. The miracle, too, that the God who called Abram also calls us every single day into an adventure of significance, into lives that matter, into lives that make a difference.

Lives of promise, of promises given, waiting to be fulfilled.

How do we know for sure?

Because God promised.

TRAVELING MERCY

Dear one,
I'm interrupting the broadcast
That is your life
To invite you into mine,
Into real life,
Into faith and hope.
Are you ready?
This is your genesis,
Your new start,
The beginning-again
Possible only with me.
A yes today
Will change
All your tomorrows.
What do you say?

NOTE TO SELF

Today I begin my book of beginnings again. And tomorrow.

NOTE

1. There is some question about when Abram's father, Terah, actually died. If he had Abram at age seventy (Gen. 11:26) and died at 205, and if Abram left Harran at age seventy-five (Gen. 12:4), then Terah lived another sixty years after Abram answered God's call with a "Yes." However, Stephen in Acts 7:4 tells us that Abram left after Terah's death. It is possible that Stephen referenced the Samaritan Pentateuch, which shows that Terah died at age 145. (Gleaned from *English Standard Version Study Bible*)

MARCH 2

HEARING THE CALL

The LORD had said. . . .
—GENESIS 12:1

The whole idea of God calling us forces questions and offers few definite answers. It both frightens and intrigues us. What if we don't hear the call? Or don't recognize it? What if we can't answer with yes? Or don't want to? What if God calls us to a country thousands of miles away to be a missionary? What if God calls us to do something dreadfully difficult, or something that doesn't line up with our current lifestyle? What if God's call embarrasses us, or people don't confirm that call on our lives? What if people *tsk-tsk* us and shake their heads, like, "I'm sorry you're off the beam and are probably going to fail"? And what if we truly do fail?

Plus, don't we secretly believe that God only calls people who are super godly? Or, maybe we aren't sure that God actually still calls people today. Because, isn't it a little eerie when someone says, "God has called me to do this"? Is that a literal voice or an internal sense, or are they just singing some loony tunes and in need of some meds?

But the intriguing part is the "what if." What if this call is real and God really antes up and moves and blesses? It's beyond anything we can imagine. And that's why yes is such a powerful response. We miss out on the mystery and the miraculous if we answer otherwise. People sometimes say to me, after we've spent an evening or a weekend at a retreat or conference, "People hope for their entire lives to hear God's call and to do what God calls them to do. You have found it and are doing it, and God is blessing us because of it."

I ponder this. God's call on me simply reflects the promise for every one of us: "I will bless you and make you a blessing." That's it. Out of a deep kindness greater than anything any of us deserve, God has taken who I am, who I was, all I have experienced and been, and used the journey to convert me. In that conversion, in the losing of myself and any half-formed or misshapen identity I might have had, and in the reshaping and transforming of who I am and who I have yet to become, God has blessed me. I can't say that this part of God's promise has been fun for me or for anyone close to me. I don't navigate change easily, and my shame levels are still sometimes (OK, oftentimes) toxic. And millions of miles wait between me and who God wants me to be. But in the midst of and out of all that rather painful and ongoing molding and shaping, God allows me to bless others. In fact, God promised all of us that he would bless others through us.

That's the promise: that God will bless us and make us a blessing. Never that God will simply bless us, and never that God's blessing will be an end in itself. But that through us, the world might be blessed. We are conduits for God, for God blessing others through us.

So how do we move to that place? How about a simple prayer: "God, please bless me and allow me to be a blessing. Today." And tomorrow. And the rest of our lives. And then we watch for opportunities to live into that calling.

TRAVELING MERCY
Dear one,
You will recognize my voice
Because it won't sound like yours,
And it will require
Something of you
Beyond anything you personally
Have to offer.
That's how you will know.
And then,
Do you know what else?
You will live in the middle
Of the biggest adventure of your life
With me.
What holds you back
From saying yes
Today?

NOTE TO SELF
Be willing to leave in order to receive.

MARCH 3

I WILL SHOW YOU

"Go . . . to the land I will show you."

—GENESIS 12:1

How many times in the cold night did Abram lie wide awake under the bright night sky, chew his lip, and wonder, "Am I on the right path?" How often, in the heat of the day with its blinding glare of sun, did he throw his arm over his forehead like a visor, squint, and ask, "Really? Is this right?" How many times did he have to repeat the words God said, "Go to the land I will show you"?

As many times as necessary for him to keep the caravan's wheels turning forward. As often as necessary to keep from turning back to the people and the gods and the life he'd left behind. Every single time doubt plagued him, he could remind himself, "No, no, none of that. Here's what God said: 'I will show you.'"

That's a promise. Not an "I might" or "If I am in the mood." Not, "If I can remember the route or find the map or care on that particular day." God said, "I will show you." It's a promise, and a promise is only as good as the one who makes it. We trust our bank, and our bank fails. We trust our economy, and it collapses. We trust our leaders, and they slip into a moral black hole. We trust our parents or spouse or friends, and they disappoint us. But if God promised, then doesn't that change everything? God is the bank that never fails. God is the economy that never collapses and the leader who never slips.

But to imagine that we've never likewise been disappointed by the way God answered us, or didn't answer us, would make us liars. Or at least, people who rarely reflect on the difference between hope and reality. Or on the difference between what we believe to be true and what we experience on a daily basis.

Just to be clear: At no time does what we think about God or what we experience of God change who God actually is.

Sometimes we think our journey with God depends on the power of our faith in the One who calls us forward. But that isn't true. God's faithfulness doesn't depend even remotely on the quantity or quality of our faith. God is faithful, regardless of how much or how hard we believe.

Is the problem, when it comes to following God, really our own fear of not hearing clearly? Or perhaps our own autonomy and desire to be the director of our own pathways?

Our ability to leave where we are, and our willingness to go where God leads, depends on that final phrase, "I will show you." Because if God could show Abram, then God can show us. Our job is to watch, and to keep walking. Maybe it's time to lace up those sandals.

TRAVELING MERCY
Dear one,
Here's the deal:
I called you.
I promised.
I will be faithful.
What part of that
Don't you believe?
And who has hurt you
So much that it is difficult
To believe me
Or to trust me
Or to follow me?
I am faithful
And I will be faithful,
And I will not—
Repeat, I will not—
Abandon you
On the trail.
So come with me,
Follow me,
To the land
I will show you.

NOTE TO SELF
Fear won't stop me from following God.

MARCH 4

STEP BY STEP

"Leave . . . and go to the land I will show you."
—GENESIS 12:1 NIV84

God said, "Leave," to Abram. Leave. Take off. Head out of here, now. And did Abram ask, "Whoa, wait. What? Where am I going?"

We don't know that Abram asked that aloud, asked the One who told him to go, the One he'd never heard from before in his entire life. But surely he thought it and wondered about it in the privacy of his own thoughts (as if that were possible with God), or while hidden away in the nighttime with his wife, Sarai. "Go where? What is God asking of me? How will I know if this is the right next plan for us?"

Funny how God doesn't send the entire map to Abram, or to us. Doesn't download the plan with every twist and turn en route. Funny . . . how funny that isn't. *Hahahaha*, if only we'd known about all those flat tires. That we would lose the job within months of moving. Or that something would happen to someone we love on the way. Known that it was the last time we would see so-and-so, known that the turbulence would force an emergency landing. If only we'd known.

How often would anyone say yes, if we really knew the aches and pains of faith-travel? Knew what it would cost us, in terms of blisters on our soles and on our souls, as well as on our relationships? Because a yes will cost us, too, though in different ways than a no to God's summons.

But that's just the point. If we knew, we might say no. This way, an unqualified yes leads us . . . where?

To a place God will show us. Isn't this the essence of the invitation, the best and amazing part, and the reason we can answer in the affirmative? Yes, we say. Not because we know the future, have considered how much we'll lose, and have factored in the marauding forces along the way with all the pillaging and looting and sheep-stealing, all the battles and skirmishes and plain old stupidity. And did we mention sin?

We say yes because, ultimately, we choose to trust the God we can't see rather than the life we can see.

On the way to where, again?

On the way to where God will show us. God *will* show us, just as in Abram's time. God said, "To the land I will show you."

When Abram told Sarai, "Time to pack up; time to go," she surely asked, "Go where?"

"To the land God will show us."

If it was good enough for them, then it's enough for me. Enough for me to say yes, in spite of all the unknowns that constrict my throat and clutch at my chest. In spite of the risks involved. In spite of the good-byes and I-love-yous that I will have to say to others in order to say yes to God.

Because if God is calling us to freedom, whatever terrain we encounter, then God will take us there. Step by step by desert step.

TRAVELING MERCY
Dear one,
Do you hear me calling?
Calling you to leave.
But not just to leave,
To follow me.
I will show you the land,
And we will call the land
Freedom,
The land of promise,
The Promised Land.
Because I promised,
And I delight
To fulfill my promises.
So . . . is that your fear
Or a yes I hear?

NOTE TO SELF
Today, walk through problems into God's promise.

MARCH 5

OPPOSITE DIRECTIONS

> The LORD had said to Abram, "Leave your country, your people and your father's household and go to the land I will show you."
>
> —GENESIS 12:1 NIV84

The two words focus in opposite directions and constantly strain against one another unless we resolve the tension. "Leave," God said. And then, "Go." Both words, *leave* and *go*, are essential to faithfulness and to following God, vital to finding the promise. *Leave* is a backward look, a look all around us for context. What and whom are we to leave behind? What are the costs involved? If we go without recognizing what we're taking leave of, we short-change the blessings of the leaving process.

Where have we seen God's hand in *this* place? What memories, what gifts, what provisions? Because surely God has been in this place, even though we sometimes see and seek God's hand through a haze of hurt. Where have we experienced God's presence, miraculous intervention, answered prayers, joy and peace, and comfort and safety? What were the surprises of a life of faith, right here in this land we aim to leave? To cite evidence of God's goodness in the past enables us to look to God for the future.

But we can't leave legitimately, with integrity, without also asking what pains and problems exist here. This serves as both a reality check and a blessing check, enabling us to be honest down the road. The check-and-balance of leaving prevents us from over-glorifying the past: Didn't we have it good there? Wasn't that grass green, the skies never cloudy all day? Weren't our friends, our church, our jobs absolutely the best? Wasn't that just the most perfect, weed-free, unblemished time in our lives?

It might have been as perfect as anything or any place we've experienced in our journey so far, but an honest assessment includes both the flourishing gardens and the crabgrass in our own backyard. So don't forget about that tragedy, or the crisis that one year. Remember that sadness? That disappointment? We have to know what we leave behind in order to leave well. But we don't stop there: What have we learned from this place, about God, about ourselves, about life? In what ways has this place and time shaped us? Is it possible that we hear God's voice and his calling through pain as well as pleasure?

Sometimes, difficult situations instigate our leaving—a job loss, a crushed relationship, or a collapsed dream—and how easy to leave with bitterness and blame, overlooking any blessings of this era. Leaving well, with an honest appraisal, stops us from saying from a flat-lined soul, "Good riddance. I leave nothing of worth behind." We can try to shake the dust off our feet, but it will harden to mud and weigh down our steps with unshed tears and unexpressed losses later on.

Of course it might seem easier to just leave, because then we escape without public display of emotions like grief and disappointment. Or to leave without resolution of the angst, the anger, the awfulness that sometimes leads us to the moving van. We see this in churches: People leave behind a lifetime of memories because of a current pain or problem and just disappear. Pastors exit a church without a celebration of both the divine and the difficult, and both church and pastoral family lose out on closure, but also on the blessing.

"Leave," God had said. "Leave your country, your people, your father's household." We have to know what we leave behind in order to move forward with a clean chalkboard of anticipation, ready for God to write on our life slate with new events and new encounters.

TRAVELING MERCY
Dear one,
With me
You can be honest.
If we are to leave well
Together,
Then we leave well
By being clear.
It's been hard
And it's been good,
And if you look closely
You will see my faithfulness
In the land you leave behind.
But that faithfulness you will never
Leave behind,
Because I will show you
To the next land.

NOTE TO SELF
Leave well by learning from the past.

MARCH 6

PICK TWO

"Leave . . . and go . . . and I will bless you."
—GENESIS 12:1–2 NIV84

Leave and go. How tempting it is to always either be leaving (looking behind) or going (looking ahead), rather than to be staying in the right now and living here in the meantime. In all the work of our personal travel toward wholeness and holiness, in the daily ins-and-outs of our lives, being here right now seems impossible. So much drama and so many issues surround us. So much *going* going on. And whether in an office or a factory, or in our own homes, to some degree we are in charge of getting others going and getting them where they're going.

Regardless of where we've been and where we're headed, we are always somewhere, right now, and the crux of our journey is that the right now be the best, most attentive now possible. Otherwise, we miss the actual living of our lives. In the world's eyes, perhaps, our life's work is about going, about accomplishing. Innovation and inventiveness are rewarded, inertia not so much. We get "paid" for making things happen, not typically for guarding the status quo. And then one day we look up and don't remember how we got to this point in our lives because we live in a time zone called "next," rather than "now."

Sometimes I pull into my driveway and wonder how I got home. I don't remember the route, the stoplights, whether there was a train on the tracks. . . . I was zoned out, driving carefully (one hopes) but robotically, without noticing. Living life on automatic with the accelerator pressed down means we lose out on living. The scenery flashes past before we can focus.

Perhaps this is one reason behind resting on the seventh day—so we notice our life today, the people we love, the God who loves us. At least on this one day we aren't trekking after the great bottom line or the next goal in the game. We are present in the moment, in the day. In that reveling, we stop unraveling and begin to mend.

And begin to marvel. "Look," we exclaim, "at the shoots of green pushing through the dead leaves!" Or we really hear a child's delightful laugh, and our heart leaps. Maybe we notice for the first time that our heart has a "resting rate," which we don't appreciate in our great race forward.

We hear God say, "Leave." Oh, we are mastering the "Go" part. And we want to believe the promise that follows: "I will bless you." But when we focus on the "I *will* bless you," we forget that God's blessing isn't just future tense. It is present tense. God is blessing us now, and one day, today's blessing will be folded into tomorrow's stories about yesterday. So we pay attention, in between the leaving and the going, and realize that we are really living. Today.

TRAVELING MERCY
Dear one,
Right now is the only time
That really matters
In the long run
That is your life.
Trust me enough
In between
Your obedient leaving and going
To live in the right now.
I will bless you;
I am blessing you,
And would love
To notice that with you.
Right now.

NOTE TO SELF
Stop the unraveling by beginning to revel.

MARCH 7

REDEFINING

"And I will bless you."
—Genesis 12:2

Recognizing God's blessing requires a new lens. The blessing might not look like we hope or perhaps have been led to believe it should look: the new job, new car, new relationship. It might not resemble the signs of status or success that our world reveres. An unofficial definition of *blessing* in some people's dictionary might be "prosperity." But, in fact, it mostly means a verbal encouragement or praise or glorifying. A consecration, or setting apart. To bless is to bestow favor in the sense of regard or respect.

Maybe, just maybe, I've used this word incorrectly from the beginning of my spiritual journey. In church lingo, *blessing* is either something you say over the food or the idea of God giving us stuff. Or we pray, "Lord, bless this . . ." (fill in the blank: meeting, group, family, event, task). What do we mean when we pray that prayer? Don't we mean that all will go well, or that God's Spirit will be present, or both?

All might not go well, but, if so, that isn't an un-blessing. Blessing actually means that God sees us and loves us. God confers on us a level of grace. It's quite a miracle, inexplicable in a world where you get what you paid for, and we haven't any pocket change.

As I mulled over this new definition of blessing, I started to listen throughout the day for the usage of the word. At a lunch meeting, I enthused over something good that happened in a member's life: "This is such a blessing." As I left the restaurant, the waiter murmured, "Thank you. God bless you," with a bow of his head. Automatically, I repeated to him, "God bless you, too."

A woman in the group asked over her shoulder, "What did you mean when you said, 'God bless you'?"

Along with, "What did I mean?" I should ask, "Did I mean it?"

My unofficial poll of friends and acquaintances on social media, which asked them, "What do you mean when you ask God to bless . . . ?" generated the most responses of any of my polls (with the exception of one about chocolate). Most people were essentially asking God to do good in people's lives, whatever they need, whatever it would look like for God to do good.

Two wise word watchers said they rarely pray in such a general way. To them, asking God to "bless" is the lazy way out of specific prayer for specific people.

On the other hand, for people who are control freaks in their prayer life, constantly providing God with a long list of what to do for whom, and how soon (*ahem* . . . maybe I am a little bit like that), a general prayer might be the best solution. Letting God determine what blessing looks like in another's life is an open-handed way to pray. As though we could define that for God, anyway.

Mostly, it helps me to reconsider what blessing means, as far as God is concerned. Just because I don't have the same stuff or drive as nice a car as someone else, just because I don't have a perfect household, doesn't mean that God isn't blessing me. It doesn't mean God hasn't blessed or won't bless me. I *am* blessed, because God tells me so. "I have loved you with an everlasting love" (Jer. 31:3).

That should bless me, all the way to heaven.

TRAVELING MERCY
Dear one,
The fact of blessing is this:
That I confer on you favor,
And with that favor
A kindness that includes
Whatever I see
That you need
Right now
And down the road.
Please don't confuse the two.
And also know this:
Right now will lead you down the road,
And en route
My blessing for you
Might not look like another's blessing.
So know this—
I love you,
And I know.

NOTE TO SELF
Look up, not around, to define blessing.

MARCH 8

JUST GREAT

"I will make your name great."
—GENESIS 12:2

God told Abram, "I will make your name great." Leave your greatness up to me, God said. This removed enormous responsibility and temptation from Abram, and removes it from us, as well. God gets to both define *great* and bring great to pass. Note the critical order of God's calling of Abram:

1. Leave
2. Go
3. I will show you
4. I will make you into a great nation
5. I will bless you
6. I will make your name great
7. You will be a blessing

The greatness required of Abram was the greatness of submission. God asked Abram to obey, then to leave and follow. And then God took responsibility for the rest. "I will . . ." God said.

We seek greatness in various ways: business, sports, volunteerism, politics, relationships. To leave our greatness in God's hands, and to leave it up to God to define, requires faith. But how much riskier for us to define for ourselves what a great name looks like. Risky because then the temptation grows to make greatness happen on our time and through our own power. Risky because renown feeds into the constantly draining pool of self-esteem that requires unending replenishment.

When we attempt to both define greatness and bring it to pass, we can end up comparing ourselves to others—to their apparent accomplishments and what we consider to be their blessings. No one wins the lottery of comparison. There are always more apples on the neighbors' trees or better cars in their garage, and discontent becomes our distressing and hand-wringing companion.

Then, too, greatness as an end in itself is like a match lit in a roomful of natural gas. We can expect problems and even explosions when we try to make greatness happen on our own terms. Didn't Satan use this as a temptation with Jesus in the wilderness, luring him with a view of all the kingdoms of the world? "I will give you all their authority and splendor . . . if you worship me" (see Luke 4:5–8). Whether greatness looks like power, prestige, progeny, or plain old prosperity, if we think we're the ones who make our names great, we can land in a heap of trouble. In the pursuit of greatness, compromised ethics can collapse economies. Moral and often financial ruin can accompany the greatness chase, because of the great insatiable tagalong, greed.

Life spins out of control when greatness is our solo goal.

But if our life goal is to leave and go, to leave behind us in the dust our own shallow desires and dreams in order to follow God, then the responsibility for greatness is God's.

Maybe, then, the question we should ask ourselves is, "Greatness in whose eyes?" While we constantly search others' eyes for approval, all that really matters is greatness in God's eyes. And the root of greatness? Obedience. Greatness redefined might be simply following God. Then it is God's greatness that gets the glory, rather than any effort on our part.

That's it. The recipe for greatness, the great secret of the ages.

It might be harder—and easier— than we ever imagined.

TRAVELING MERCY
Dear one,
This is a most exciting
Part of the journey.
We head out together,
But I get to make your name
Great.
I get to define how that greatness looks
And how it impacts the world.
And won't you be surprised
To recognize
My hand
Guiding you
And blessing you.

If your goal is simply to
Follow me,
Then all will be well;
In fact,
It will be
Great.

NOTE TO SELF
God defines greatness, and I will follow God.

MARCH 9

THE GREAT DANGER

"I will make your name great."
—Genesis 12:2

At seventy-five, did Abram suddenly feel a need to have a great name? Probably not. But clearly something changed him. Imagine getting an adrenaline rush at that age that powers your journey for the rest of your life. (Especially considering all the miles he would log before his sons laid his old bones to rest in the cave with his beloved wife at the earthly end of that journey.) Rather than simply being inspired by a human longing for greatness, it would seem that the personal invitation to follow God must have been so compelling that Abram decided that age was irrelevant. Unlike so much in our society, God's calling is not discriminatory against age.

Whether from our admiration of celebrities from Hollywood or sports, heroes from larger-than-life stories, or headliners on news magazines, we have our own definition of greatness as embodied by others. Yet rarely do we feel we exemplify that adjective ourselves. Someone else is great, or at least greater. Always someone else. Never us.

But great is dangerous. Greatness can ruin you. Look at some of our sports greats: accused of murder, abuse, gambling, or throwing games. Look at celebrity brawls, whether from Hollywood or Wall Street or the political power players. Look at the tragedies that often come with greatness: divorce, desperation, the destruction of family and career with one bad move. A world-defined greatness is often just greed: greediness for power, for money, for the next high.

Mikhail Baryshnikov, the famous ballet dancer who defected from the Soviet Union, spoke at my son's college graduation. He challenged the seniors to not worry about being "the best." Best is a superlative someone else ascribes to you, he said. An external label. Rather, he suggested, strive to describe yourself as "better." Better at dance, better at music, better at acting. Better at whatever course you choose to follow. Better at serving others. Better at life.

Better is something only we can choose. And we can choose better every single day. "How are you?" someone asks. And we answer, "Better, thank you."

Hopefully they will ask a follow-up question, like, "Better? Were you ill?"

"No, not at all. I'm getting better at following God. I'm getting better at loving my neighbor. I'm getting better at my craft. Better. Every single day."

"Better" is a much better personal goal than greatness. Then we are free to leave the greatness up to God.

TRAVELING MERCY

Dear one,
My calling of you
Isn't dependent on you at all;
It depends on me
And my love for you
And the plans I anticipate
For you.
Hear that?
For you.
And that means,
You'll get to grow
Better every day
At paying attention,
Better every day
At loving,
Better every day
At serving.
That's true greatness.

NOTE TO SELF
What does better look like today?

MARCH 10

THE GREATNESS FACTOR

"I will make your name great."
—Genesis 12:2

For years, I've been included in an industry that thrives on people's great names, and the greater the name, the greater *everything* for everyone involved. Likely most careers are like this: the greater the name, the greater the reward, the greater the incentive to become even greater. During this stretch of time, I've met people who truly had great names. God had blessed them in all the officially sanctioned forms of blessing, and they'd become a blessing to millions of people.

But, through the years, the cost to some of those people, in terms of pressure to keep meeting an externally imposed mandate of greatness, was enough to shatter them. Some suffered nervous breakdowns. For others, the necessity of producing yet another superlative work crippled them creatively. Still others, who tried faithfully to cooperate with the greatness, hired staff and expanded ministry horizons and spent more and more money. Keeping up with the greatness cost more and more. They were home less and less, often sleeping in hotels twenty times a month. This with a family at home. Others split the greatness with someone else, but when the partnership dissolved were stuck with enormous expenses, debt, and obligations.

That kind of greatness would have destroyed both me and my family. Even though held up as the ideal (and sometimes the idol) in our industry, that level of household "name-ism" requires more than I could have given. I see now in retrospect, and with a lungful of relief and gratitude, that God saved us.

I wish I'd understood sooner the key element of Abram's story, of God's calling to Abram and the promises made. Although I don't know if I would have listened or believed it. Nowhere did God say, "You head off and make a name for yourself, so you can make me proud." Rather, God said, "I will make your name great." As we try to be faithful to God's call on our lives, we can let our reputation and all results rest with God.

Greatness from any source other than God can maim our spirit and our relationship with God and others. Then factor in what that does to our relationship with ourselves, with what we know deep down on the inside about our personal non-greatness and what we have to show to others to keep up our great image. Trying to become who others think we should be according to some false manual of greatness separates us from the center of our being, from God who wants to be our center. It is one of the sorrier faces of codependence and dysfunction, a deep-rooted cause of misery and moral breakdown.

Defined by anyone other than God, greatness becomes slavery. As an end in itself, greatness is the most deplorable of goals. Greatness is a voracious monster that demands more and better food. Ultimately, greatness becomes a sort of auto-immune disease, where the body tries to kill itself off. It will consume us, if we aren't mindful.

Perhaps mindfulness is one of the paths to true greatness. Mindfulness of our own feebleness and foibles, awareness that in us resides no good thing. That left to ourselves, we would descend to depravity and take our supposed greatness and our loved ones with us.

Mindfulness, too, of God's astounding acceptance of us, this God who knows all the fractures within ourselves and still says, "It's very good."

Maybe, beyond any label anyone else attaches to us, that is a secret to greatness: that God has called us good and that called us. Out of that declaration we live, greatly mindful of passing along that affirmation to others.

TRAVELING MERCY
Dear one,
Greatness has never been your job
Just as it was never Abram's job.
All I ask of you
Is to follow me,
And to be mindful
Of your weakness,
Yes,
But also of my world-sized
Love for you.
My goodness is enough
For you.
It is big enough,
Wide enough,

High enough,
Deep enough.
It is enough.
So enough of this worry
About greatness.
I love you,
And that should be enough.

NOTE TO SELF
God is great, and that's good enough for me.

MARCH 11

A ROUND

"I will bless those who bless you."
—Genesis 12:3

Genesis 12:2–3 is a beautiful circular blessing. God blessed Abram, who blessed others, which caused others to bless Abram, and God blessed the people who blessed Abram. The cycle of blessing never ends, this gift that keeps giving and giving and costs us so very little. Except perhaps our pride, because to continue to show favor to others requires humility on our part. As does acceptance of others in spite of evidence that they don't merit any favor whatsoever.

Anonymity makes it easier to disrespect another, to withhold favor. Road rage isn't typically directed at someone an angry driver already knows, but against a stranger. The lack of relationship lowers our expectations of ourselves, and we forget our manners. We don't worry about ruining our reputation with someone who doesn't know us, because we have no history with that person. Lack of relationship can lead to risky behavior, to un-blessing. Relationship generates respect.

But blessing others isn't contingent upon our relationship with them. Abram knew absolutely no one from the future when

God said, "You will be a blessing." Blessing, regardless of preexisting relationships, is a directive from God. Plus, if God says to bless others, it isn't because they necessarily deserve a blessing. Who does, after all, deserve a blessing? It is a divinely granted gift, nothing earned or deserved.

Once (OK, possibly more than once) in the security of my car with all the windows closed, I flew into a tirade against the person driving in front of me. In my hurry to get nowhere important, people's incompetence behind their steering wheels drove me up the wall.

Then I imagined my parents, both octogenarians and beyond, driving the car ahead of me. How would I want a driver following them to act? In a rage? Or with kindness? My blood pressure instantly lowered and shame crept into my soul. The simple act of imagining myself in relationship with the other person entirely changed both my acceptance of and my attitude toward them.

We remember our manners when we stop to recognize our kinfolk in the house next door, the car in front of us, the person in the airplane seat alongside us. We reset our expectations of them, as well as of ourselves.

When we realize that, initially and even ultimately, we are related to one another, it allows us to bless them, no matter what. And people who are blessed are so surprised by the blessing that they in turn pass along a blessing. Perhaps to us, perhaps to others. Either way, it's hard to say who is most blessed.

Then again, aren't we, the ones who bless, the most blessed? Isn't that what Jesus said? "Freely you have received; freely give" (Matt. 10:8). We receive blessing, we give blessing. So today, how about it? "It is more blessed to give than to receive" (Acts 20:35). Let's set in motion the endless cycle of blessing.

TRAVELING MERCY

Dear one,
Please
Remember your manners,
Your pleases and thank-yous,
And remember that if I love you
Then I also love the people
You encounter.
So please
Love them in the way I love you,
And the blessing
Will go on and on
And on.
To the end of the age.

NOTE TO SELF

Today I will bless forward.

MARCH 12

WORLDVIEW

"Through your offspring all peoples on earth will be blessed."
—Acts 3:25

Fast forward a couple thousand years from Abram's initial intersection with the calling and the promise. Peter and John, followers of a Jewish man many acknowledged as the Messiah, headed to the temple for afternoon prayers. A man carried a crippled beggar to the temple gate, a gate ironically called Beautiful. The man laid down his burden and disappeared into the crowd.

But the man on the pallet, the crippled beggar, looked up from ground level at the two men who hustled toward the gate and the temple. The beggar fancied a handout, a few pennies to get through yet another day. He asked for money, never expecting the miracle headed his way.

Peter and John stared at him, then said, "Look at us!" The beggar did, hand outstretched. Peter said, "Silver or gold I do not have, but what I have I give you. In the name of Jesus Christ of Nazareth, walk." He then gripped the man's hands and pulled him to his feet. The beggar leaped and jumped and turned cartwheels into the temple with Peter and John.

This created quite a ruckus, all that celebrating. The people were floored by the healing—imagine, crippled from birth and now dancing in the streets!—and came running (see Acts 3:1–10). Peter sized up the crowd, seized the moment, and brought them up to speed. He quoted, from all the vast quantities of Scripture he could access, about God's promise through Abraham. Of course, of course the miracle came from God, from the man Jesus.

"Why does this surprise you?" Peter asked. "The God of Abraham . . . has glorified his servant Jesus" (Acts 3:12–13). After all, you should've been expecting this all along, because God said to Abraham, back there in Harran, "All the peoples on earth will be blessed through you."

Peter shook up the normal interpretation of this, which is that Abraham would have a great big family that would spread out and bless the world and allow us to sing songs like, "Father Abraham had many sons . . . " Peter quoted God's covenant with Abraham from Genesis 12:2–3: "Through your offspring all peoples on earth will be blessed." Peter reframed the entire history of God's calling and the promised blessing: The whole wide world will be blessed through your offspring, Jesus.

Including who? The whole world! The entire world would be blessed by Abram's offspring—through Jesus. Including this crippled beggar at the gate called Beautiful. Including the crippled beggars like me, like you. And that day at the gate called Beautiful, the One who said, "I am the gate," removed the barriers and began the business of blessing through us.

TRAVELING MERCY
Dear one,
I told you
The song that never
Ends but begins
Always
With blessing,
Through my servant Abraham,
Through my Son Jesus,
Through you,
My child.
Is that dancing I hear?
The sound of celebration?
Sing on.

NOTE TO SELF
The blessing is for and through beggars like me.

MARCH 13

NEVER TOO LATE

> "I will make you into a great nation, and I will bless you;
> I will make your name great, and you will be a blessing. I will
> bless those who bless you, and whoever curses you I will curse;
> and all peoples on earth will be blessed through you."
>
> —Genesis 12:2–3

Hurtling through the sky at 489 miles per hour, I pulled my journal from my briefcase and began to write my prayers. Maybe, like me, you've been praying and praying for days and weeks and months and years for someone to catch fire with God, or for healing, or repentance, or growth. And, like me, you sometimes despair that it is just too late.

As I prayed for people I love, some of whom I don't even know—prayed for their healing and their disappointments, their wrong turns and chronic pain and diseases and broken hearts—I stuttered in my prayers. Their ages run the range of the year-long temperatures (and it's been a record-hot summer after a cold and snowy winter), and my own heart squeezed in pain. Maybe it's just too late. Too late for love, too late for healing, too late for hope and for new spiritual adventures. Maybe their hearts are too hard and their patterns too entrenched, regardless of their current decade of life.

On the plane, as pain squished my heart in its vise-like grip, I turned to my weekly Scripture reading, starting in Genesis 12.

I read, my soul throbbing back to life, about this great faith adventure: "The LORD had said to Abram, 'Go from your country, your people and your father's household to the land I will show you. I will make you into a great nation, and I will bless you; I will make your name great, and you will be a blessing . . . and all peoples on earth will be blessed through you.'"

Abram had never heard of this God, and yet, the passage says, "So Abram went, as the LORD had told him; and Lot went with him. Abram was seventy-five years old when he set out from Harran."

Wait. What? I reread the last verse. Seventy-five? That's a winter-time thermostat setting. He packed up all his possessions, his beautiful childless wife, Sarai, and his rather troublesome relative, Lot. He saddled up and followed this unknown God, who hadn't yet established for Abram a track record of faithfulness. Packed up and headed out on an exploration that would change the world.

My heart thumped. Does this kind of promise hold for us? All of us, and the people we love, thousands of years removed from almost-octogenarian Abram? I fretted over this, then turned to the next passage in my weekly set of Scriptures. Romans 4:16–17 popped in my soul like the top on a carbonated drink: "Therefore, the promise comes by faith, so that it may be by grace and may be guaranteed to all Abraham's offspring—not only to those who are of the law but also to those who have the faith of Abraham. He is the father of us all. As it is written: 'I have made you a father of many nations.'" Does the promise hold true today? A resounding yes, God said.

All the peoples on the earth will be blessed through Abraham, and then through us.

This set my heart wagging again. I watched the airplane's progress on the screen in front of me. We flew at thirty-two thousand feet with Tokyo as our destination. There I would minister around Japan with people from many nations.

With my heart pumping and a smile pushing clear into my cheeks, I returned to my prayers. It's never too late to head into an adventure with God. Not for me, nor for you. Not for those we love. The promise, indeed, holds.[1]

TRAVELING MERCY
Dear one,
Now do you believe me?
My promise holds,
My word is true;
I know the future
And have huge plans for you.
Your legacy will endure,
And if you will just trust me
And follow me,
I have a promise
And a plan just for you.
The adventure is ever before us,
Ageless.

NOTE TO SELF
It's never too late for blessing.

NOTE
1. This devotional first appeared in *Indeed* magazine, May/June 2012, 6–7.

MARCH 14

STEPPING AWAY FROM THE CYCLE

> "I will bless those who bless you,
> and whoever curses you I will curse."
>
> —Genesis 12:3

Ever wonder how often Abram referred back to this part of God's promise? God blesses, we bless in response, and God covers for us if others curse us. What an idea: Abram didn't need to worry his shaggy gray head about how others perceived him. Wouldn't this be a terrific way to live, totally free of the need to correct others' impressions of us or their opinions about us?

Moving past the idea that another's belief about us defines us may be called spiritual maturity, emotional intelligence, and even freedom from codependence. Codependence often lays down a shame base, creating the foundation for a self-destructing house of cards built on opinion and misimpression and judgment from others. For isn't that what it is when another curses us? Cursing casts judgment.

And most of us have been in positions where we've been judged, weighed, and found wanting. We've come under the microscope of scrutiny and had our defects examined and exposed. Our failures are real, but the disclosure and accusation feels poisonous. It feels so bad that we may want to defend ourselves or cast about for word-bombs to hurl back across the boundary line, something to even the score again and let our critics know they are also defective, hopefully worse than we are.

Another's judgment can feel wretched, because however right they may be about our faults, we are still human beings created for life and blessing. And sometimes, in our deepest, most wounded base nature, we do want to hurt another for hurting us.

But reverse this whole thought process for a minute. What if we wear the other shoe, rather than the one with the bomb in it?

God says, "I will bless you and make you a blessing, and I will bless those who bless you." Our primary and perhaps only job description is to bless. Cursing, the other role, is left entirely up to God. (Note: This does not give others permission to abuse us, whether verbally, physically, or emotionally, nor does the passage suggest that we sit still and allow that to happen.)

This promise from God frees us from vindictiveness, from wanting to hurt those who hurt us, which is in the same vein as judging those who judge us. If we curse others, then we remove ourselves from the cycle of blessing.

Cursing another—can't this take many forms, from gossip to bad-mouthing to actually swearing at another person, cursing takes us out of the blessing wheel. Plus, when we curse another, we put ourselves in the role of God. This has been our problem since the days of Adam and Eve, revealing the core of our sin nature: wanting to be like God.

God knows the pain others cause us. He knows that our reactions are often based on our own longing to be safe and loved. And God is the only one who can reassure us. So today, when my mouth starts to disassociate from my common sense and also from my primary calling, if I can't bless with my words and actions, I will shut my mouth and open my heart to God.

And leave the rest up to him.

TRAVELING MERCY
Dear one,
Your opinion of yourself,
Your "self-esteem,"
Has nothing to do with you
Or what others say about you.
Who you are is based entirely
On what I say about you.
So own the pain
Another causes you,
But step away
From the temptation to hurt in response
And settle back
Into my promise.
I will bless,
You will bless,
And I will take care of any differences.

NOTE TO SELF
Today I will bless, process, and bless again.

MARCH 15

START THE BALL ROLLING

So Abram went.

—GENESIS 12:4

God's instructions to Abram, to leave and go, start the overarching theme of the Pentateuch, the first five books of the Scriptures. These books chronicle the constant travel of a nation's worth of people, their leaving and going. But an even larger theme resonates: God's blessing. When Abram chose to follow God's lead, God promised to bless Abram, to make of him a great nation, and to bless others through him. Isn't this the basis for all our lives? How might this become the theme of our lives, the great undergirding on which we frame our homes of faith? We need to redirect our focus.

God said, "You need to get out of Babylon, evacuate Harran, and go to a land I will show you."

I will show you.

You don't choose the land.

You don't make a name for yourself.

You don't let your life revolve around yourself.

You don't protect yourself or your future.

God's promises don't revolve around our efforts. Rather, our trust revolves around God's promises. Abram's motives didn't have to be factored into the mix, nor did his sense of direction or lack thereof. He didn't need to read a map or worry about where his next footstep would strike. Abram's sole responsibility was to take God's favor and offer it to others. However that favor looked, whatever blessing rolled out and showed up, Abram was to bless others, to favor others.

Ah, so this is how greatness reveals itself—in the way we treat others.

One of the happiest countries in the world, the Kingdom of Bhuton in the Himalayas, reimagined their Gross National Product to become, instead, Gross National Happiness. They ask of any new policy or law, "What effect does this have on our people? On our environment?"[1] Studies find that the happiest people include people who serve others, whose lives create positive impact on other people's lives. Of what value is fame or fortune or the biggest fishing boat on the lake if we live a life of no use to others?

In spite of how we actually live, at no point should our lives revolve around ourselves. This challenge strikes at our basic need for self-protection and preservation, at the sometimes-essential egocentric patterns of so much of our lives. But with basic survival needs met, can't we free up our emotional energies to decentralize our focus?

Doesn't Scripture back this up? Jesus, when his disciples wanted to know who would be the greatest in the kingdom, said, "The greatest among you is the one who serves."

I will bless you, God says. And you will be a blessing. Not you might be, or you ought to be, or I wish you would be. But "you *will* be a blessing."

TRAVELING MERCY

Dear one,
And so will you be a blessing
And watch the impact
That blessing has
On this entire world.
Imagine a village of people
Who practice blessing.
Imagine a state's worth of people
Who practice blessing.
Imagine a world full
Of people who practice
Blessing.
And then you find
That you are imagining
Heaven
Right here on earth.
So start today.
What are we waiting for?

NOTE TO SELF
Decentralize. Find ways to bless others today.

NOTE

1. *The Happy Movie*, directed by Roko Belik (Universal City, CA: Shady Acres, 2011), DVD.

MARCH 16

DESERT IDENTITY

So Abram went, as the Lord had told him.
—Genesis 12:4

"So Abram went," the record tells us. God said leave and go. Abram left. Abram went. The actual leaving is such a big step, and although we may think we have left well, we have no idea how much our identity depends on what we've left behind, until we leave it behind us. We leave behind so much of our context.

When Abram left his father's household, he left behind everything that secured his future. To leave meant giving up all stake in any inheritance Terah might bequeath him. It meant severing relationships, leaving people he might never see again and likely wouldn't even hear from again.

That's a lot of leaving, a lot of staking faith on the promises of a God he'd never heard of before. But supposedly Abram examined the costs and still tied on his sandals and strapped his belongings onto a cart. He wrapped his arms around his brother, his sisters-in-law, all the nieces and nephews, and said good-bye.

No doubt the household of Terah shook their collective heads, sighed deep into their beards, and wondered if Abram had lost his mind. Maybe the desert heat had finally addled his thinking.

Like Abram, if we listen to that push, to the pull ahead command and beckoning of God, the scaffolding of our life starts to fall away. Sometimes in leaving our context we discover who we really are. And, who we really aren't. So much of our life's meaning comes from what we do, and to leave that behind and step out into the unsure and uncertain dismantles our identity.

There, we knew what to do, knew at least somewhat who we were within the parameters of relationship and activity. Knew our spheres of belonging and our roles within those spheres. Now, we may not be sure what even to hope for, and we are left with an unsettling look at our unadorned life and soul. Our reactions and motives become more obvious, and our relationship with God and others may strain under the big, and getting bigger, revelations about our own insecurities and insufficiencies.

We move forward toward the promise and in a sense lose our life. But what choice do we have? To step into God's call means that we have to step away from something else and into the unseen, the unknown. It means leaving behind some of who we were in order to find out who God wants us to be, and to become.

After all, to follow God's call might not mean a literal move. Nothing might change in terms of job or house. No yard sales, no moving vans. No passports, visas, or foreign countries. But following God always means an internal change, and navigating that change with our earthly compass is impossible. We like charts and timetables, phone numbers to call, services to enlist. This gives us marching orders and a plan. But our interior landscape defies calculations and flowcharts. To pursue God's call we need the work of the Spirit.

Following God is, first and ultimately, an inside job. An inside job that changes us. If we could take a before and after shot, what would be different about us? What part of yourself is God calling you to leave behind? And what part is God asking you to grow into? Going will always mean growing.

TRAVELING MERCY

Dear one,
All the outside
Is really about the inside,
About becoming who
You are created to be.
Because when you do
Follow me,
You will become
The best you possible.
Of course you're not enough.
Of course your insufficiencies
Get triggered.
Of course you will doubt.
But don't worry;
Leave behind
The baggage
And you'll be free
To grow into
Your best you.
Because going
Means growing.

NOTE TO SELF
If I find myself in God I will never lose my identity.

MARCH 17

LET THE ADVENTURE BEGIN

Abram was seventy-five years old when he set out from Harran.
—GENESIS 12:4

"What a joke," Abram must have thought every day of his married life. Every time he signed his name, every time he pulled up accounts listed in that name, every time someone hollered, "Abram!" from across the street, did he flinch? Did men on the street corner elbow one another each time Abram walked by and whisper behind their hands, "Go figure. Poor bloke." What a cruel joke given him at birth. His father, optimist that he was, gave his newborn son a name that meant "exalted father." Perfect for building a family dynasty.

Perfect until Abram said "I do" to a woman named Sarai. The first thing we know about her was the single detail standing in the way of Abram's living up to his name. She was barren, and in case we didn't get it the first time, the Scriptures go on to say, "She had no children" (Gen. 11:30 NET).

So when God said to Abram, "I will make you into a great nation," the promise might have elicited either delight or disbelief. Abram could have snorted and then broken into a jolly laugh. "Nice one, very nice. Excellent joke." Or he could have turned his back and gone about his business, shaking his head, and muttering, "Really, God? Sarai barren all these years; we're both old enough to park in a rocking chair for the rest of our lives and you intend to make me into a great nation? In what ways Lord? And how, exactly?"

Facts really block our view of faith. How much simpler to believe and trust when the calling lines up logically with the details of our lives. For instance, common sense says that God makes a great nation out of an entire family of people, with lots and lots of babies. Population growth leads toward expansion which, depending on the people's choices, could lead to greatness. This is no real stretch of the imagination, given enough time and some good leadership. A certain amount of integrity and morality in the mix helps.

But when the promise is preposterous at best, how hard is it to explain such a zany calling to our peers? At the risk of sounding zany ourselves. Then the locals could add to their derision by circling their pointed fingers toward their temples, rolling their eyes, and muttering, "*Loco*."

But God's word and promise rely on God, not on apparent facts. Not on all the little details of our lives like, say, barrenness in the only family invited on the trip. Isn't it just like God to stack all the cards against possibility to make a promise impossible to meet by human standards? Take a man and a woman nearing their walker and wheelchair and extra-wide doorway years, throw in lifelong infertility, and then declare that you're going to make this barren couple into a great nation.

Abram said yes to the greatest adventure of his life. Abram took this out-of-the-blue God and the promise literally. In spite of the facts. He packed his bags, loaded up his wagons, rounded up the animals, and caravanned out of Harran. Abram didn't rely on the facts, but on faith in this inscrutable One who called from out of nowhere with a promise too good to be true but too unexpected not to be true.

His adventure was just about to get rolling. And ours is too. Yes?

TRAVELING MERCY
Dear one,
Since when is possibility
Or probability
The single factor
In the equation of your life?
Since when does my calling
Depend remotely
On facts or figures?
I can form an entire world
Out of nothing,
Speak life into existence.
There is absolutely nothing
Too hard for me.
So forget the facts,
And don't worry about the size of your faith.
Just keep your gaze
Fixed on me
And we will see
What the future holds.
I promise
It will be a magnum
Adventure.

I delight in doing
The impossible.
You'll see.

NOTE TO SELF
My impossibles don't limit God's promises.

MARCH 18

A NEW VIEWFINDER

So Abram went, as the LORD had told him.
—GENESIS 12:4

Life seemed good enough for Abram. He had his personal little gods that he kept in his pocket, and he had his family gods, and then of course there were the gods of his people. He sure could have said, "No thanks. I'm good here. It's not perfect, but it is what it is."

Leaving, for us, is a new paradigm, a new way of looking at our life and our choices. In what ways do we settle for "this is the way it is"? Do we just shrug our shoulders in passive acceptance of our lot in life? Just because it's what we know doesn't mean we need to stay stuck in the security of a known misery or the known hideaway.

Or maybe your defense line sounds like this: "Yes, well . . . You made me so angry, or sad, or . . ." Then it's Adam and Eve all over again. It's good to understand why we react and act like we do. But no one makes us feel anything; we get to take all the credit (or discredit) for our feelings ourselves.

"This is just the way I am," we say. "You know me. Blow first, repent later. Or never." Perhaps it sounds like this: "I'm sorry, but . . ." Fill in the blank with the excuse (or would you call it a reason?). And the latter negates the former, because sorry hopefully indicates a bit or a bunch of remorse. Not much remorse happens when we excuse our behavior by blaming our personality defect. Talk about circular reasoning. Talk about a lack of integrity. If we are truly sorry for our behavior then we stop blaming our makeup and begin to take responsibility for acting better in the future. This is the ongoing, and difficult, transformation.

What if we look at Abram's leaving and decide that we will leave behind some of who we are? To leave well, we take responsibility for ourselves. Who we are, in all its negative manifestations as well as its positive ones.

Often, a literal physical relocation involves taking inventory of all our belongings. "Oh, wow. We don't need all this. I have eighteen can openers and three broken-down lawn mowers. When was the last time we used this belt sander, anyway?" What if, similarly, we take inventory of our character assets, as well as our character defects? In this way we can decide what we should leave behind.

One friend noticed that his personal choices impacted his chronic unhappiness. To leave, for him, meant revving his dopamine supply with consistent exercise and better sleep habits. He also began to consciously focus on God's overt blessings. He reports higher energy and an improved outlook on life. And his family reports that their home is a better place to live.

To leave well, we relinquish passivity and relish action. Whether internal or external action, we set in motion our personal choices and growth options.

I discovered, in one of our leavings that involved not a physical relocation but a shift in calling, that my fear overwhelms my faith constantly. The fallout was constant distraction from the people around me as well as from all the evidence of God's faithfulness. Fear became my focus and occupied the majority of my limited brain and emotional space.

Fear might be a good weight to leave behind. Although I don't think it will sell at the yard sale.

TRAVELING MERCY

Dear one,
Leave it behind.
Everything that is too heavy.
Everything that you can't carry.
The blame.
The regret.
The fear.
The grief.
The anger.
The bitterness.
The sense of failure.
I know those roots go deep,
But we can learn from them and
Then pull them out together
And start over right now.
You don't need the baggage.
And the world needs you
To be free,
To live well,
And love well.
And that's never a hard sell.

NOTE TO SELF

Today I say, "I do" to God's "I can."

MARCH 19

WAKE UP TO WONDER

So Abram left.
—Genesis 12:4 net

Maybe it's less important to consider what kind of people said yes to adventure in the past (like, Abram, venturing off into a world of flimsy tents and vagabond living), and instead focus on what it takes to say yes to today. Because we might not literally throw everything on the lawn priced to sell, then throw ourselves into our SUV and drive off into the sunset.

Rather, consider this: The nudge of God's voice to Abram speaks of newness. New voice, new calling, new life entirely. Fresh starts. Leaving yesterday behind with its misgivings and near misses to hang tattered like old flags on leaning poles.

Throughout the Scriptures, God talks about newness, "Forget the former things; do not dwell on the past. See, I am doing a new thing!" (Isa. 43:18–19). God's compassions are "new every morning" (Lam. 3:23). "See, I will create new heavens and a new earth. The former things will not be remembered, nor will they come to mind" (Isa. 65:17).

Every single day when we wake up and are not dead in the dirt is a new day, a chance to experience newness. What new thing is God going to do today? What fresh outlook or new experience of grace might head our way? What oldness can we leave behind, rather than drag into today's new start?

Each day, we get to choose: new over old, life over death, forgiveness over regret, love over anger. When Abram started plowing through the wilderness, he could have dragged the weight of all his losses. His brother's death back in Ur. Everything he left back there in the great cultured Babylonian empire. And the trek to Harran, and leaving the rest of his family there, burning the bridges of his inheritance but even more of his connections.

Abram could have headed into God's call bitter about Sarai's barrenness and the family line he didn't have. Perhaps he bristled when he bundled up Lot, his nephew, who would turn into a handful of trouble time and again down the road. Abram could have been a real bad sport about all of this.

Maybe he was. Maybe he woke up some mornings absolutely hungover with grief and loss and anger and bitterness. With fear of the future and pain over the past. Maybe you do too. But the challenge we each get, every day, is to start over. To hear God's call on our life, today, as though we'd never heard it before.

To wake up to the wonder, today, of the sun shining on our faces and God's love pouring over us. Those words, "Leave . . . and go . . . and I will make you a blessing."

This way, we always awaken on the right side of the bed.

TRAVELING MERCY

Dear one,
Good morning to you.
Good day.
Good evening.
Every second of every day
Is a new start,
A chance to awaken to the wonder
Of a world where you are loved
And you get to love.
So come on.
Get up.
Get going.
I have plans for us today —
For good not for ill,
To give you
And the world
Hope and a future.
Wake up
To the wonder.

NOTE TO SELF
Live free of yesterday and alive to today.

MARCH 20

#GROWING

> He took his wife Sarai.
> —Genesis 12:5

So far, unless we've read ahead in the story, Sarai's hashtag might read #barren or #infertile or #childless. In that society, you might also include #failure, because infertility equaled failure in one of the most important roles a woman might fulfill. In fact, bearing children was one of the only roles a woman was allowed to have, right after wifehood. Oh, add in #catastrophe to the ways to contact her, because barrenness, in those days, was that monumental of a problem.

What a recipe for barrenness of life, this labeling. How dangerous to stake our sense of self on something out of our control. The culture demanded that Sarai have babies in order to fulfill her role as a woman worth the dirt she walked on. Babies would give her a reason to get up in the morning and would earn her the "Someone Who Contributes to the World" merit badge. Plus, not only were offspring a sign of the gods' pleasure and favor, the religions of the day believed that having children somehow gave you pull in the afterlife.

She'd traveled hundreds of miles, we assume because she supposed she'd figure into Abram's blessing. But so far the record states only that Abram will be made into a mighty nation. She wasn't named, nor was a surrogate, in the initial covenant.

Maybe Sarai was just relieved to head out with her man on a new and exciting voyage. To get away from all the wives who'd succeeded at mothering. She'd already left behind the routine of Ur, with its familiar surroundings and known neighbors. There she knew her favorite vendors at the market, and knew the best civic organizations and restaurants. Sarai knew her life, back there in Ur, and she had learned to navigate Harran. No one would write a screenplay about it, but she managed to get by from day to day. Even with her #unfulfilledwoman identifier.

We might imagine her pacing and wringing her hands in her silent anxiety, a wraith dressed in black, mourning because of her barrenness, having no choice in the details or direction of her life. Or playing house-shrew, vocal about all she's given up, complaining about Abram's big dream and what it's costing her, throwing a cog of doubt into the faith wheel God set spinning.

But Sarai, by saying yes, entered the unknown. Her yes put her on the doorstep of mystery, allowing her to step away from her past and open her arms to an unexpected future. Yes defies definition and formula.

Our past shapes us, but it doesn't own us unless we allow it to. Our yes to the unknown future frees us from the grip of others' expectations. Yes means adventure. Yes means growth.

Yes opens up the world, the possibility of God creating in all new ways, ways outside of other people's regulations and expectations.

And even our own.

TRAVELING MERCY
Dear one,
No one gets to
Put a hashtag
Before your name
Except for you . . .
And except for me.
My own identifiers for you
Include, but are not limited to,
#loved
#called
#promised
#carried
#fruitful
#loved
Oh, I said that already.

NOTE TO SELF
Today, I'll call myself #yestoGodslove.

MARCH 21

DAY BY DAY

> They set out for the land of Canaan, and they arrived there.
>
> —Genesis 12:5

What happened to Abram's travelog? Don't we have a day journal of his travels, some sort of skipper's log? The Scriptures tell us "they set out" and then "they arrived." The only time that kind of directness happens for us is if we commute from desk to bathroom or some other short trek. Or else, the magnificent passage of leaving life behind, evacuating our body's shell, and transitioning to the other side, of arriving in heaven. Otherwise, we register a lot of steps on our life pedometer from here to there.

But Abram's landing in Canaan wasn't really his arrival. Because his destination, ultimately, wasn't the land. It wasn't even all the descendants God promised him. The goal wasn't about what we might consider the overt blessings at all. Abram's destination, in the long run of his life, was his faithful travel with God.

This journey—Abram's, or ours for that matter—doesn't show up on Google Maps. It's not seen in a thousand tiny veins in an atlas. It is an invisible, internal, intangible route toward becoming the person God has loved and called all along. Except, maybe the path isn't invisible or intangible after all. Because our step-by-step decisions direct our route, every single day. They sculpt our relationships every single day. For better, for worse. How we live this life of faith shapes our character, our journey, and the lives of everyone we encounter.

It's easy to minimize the tedious and plodding travel days, sunrise after sunset, attacks by bandits, empty canteens. Yawn. Same horizon, same sand, same man, same woman, day in and day out.

Isn't that true for our lives as well? It's tempting to write off huge sections of our lives, as Abram did, with, "We left" and then miraculously, suddenly, "We arrived." To leapfrog over days and weeks and years of living, particularly if they weren't noteworthy. Especially if they didn't become an enticing memoir or a riveting biopic. And certainly if we were less than stellar characters (although at least then we would have an arc to our life storyline).

Before we write off that seeming mistake, that detour; before we cross off that chunk of the journey from our life map; before we burn our travelog that shows the same old, same old us with our same old, same old reactions; before all that, let's stop. Let's remind ourselves: God sees the big picture, the entire overview of our lives and what these various days and steps and missteps and long days of sameness meant.

God knows, even when we don't. Though we can't read between the map lines of our lives for meaning, God is great at interlinear readings. So we set out.

We will arrive.

And in between, we will have some stories to tell. Today, or tomorrow. Or someday. But for today, we will try to live well, and to love well, and to listen. And maybe to take a few notes along the way. You just never know . . .

TRAVELING MERCY
Dear one,
To live deliberately
And to deliberately live
Are folded into this calling.
Today looks like tomorrow,
Looks like yesterday,
But don't let it lull you
To sleep.
Because being wakeful
Is how you move
From tedious to transformation,
From dull to delight,
From dark to light.
So wake up
And watch the sun rise,
And the Son rise
In you,
Through you
Today.

NOTE TO SELF
Today I will wake up and watch.

MARCH 22

NO PARKING ALLOWED

They set out for the land of Canaan.
—Genesis 12:5

Road trips start out as adventures, but by the corner gas station, the "How much longer?" whine leaps from everyone's tongues and drives the driver crazy. Rest stops become more frequent. And how easy would it be to lose momentum entirely and just park? For a long time. "This spot looks fine," we might say. "I could see us staying right here. Decent view. Space to spread out." Especially if we didn't know the land that awaits us. Especially if we were trying to follow a promise made with a rather vague destination. "The land I will show you," God said. Really? Is this it, yet? If not, then when? And without timetables and odometers, who knows how long the trip might take?

But when we settle down, our vision dulls and our passion dims. How do we fuel the fire of calling if we stop moving? When we settle, the fire too easily dies out. The sparks stop flying into the sky. We start to die. Weeds grow up around our tent pegs and a temporary campsite becomes a permanent home base. We sink deeper into the soil of "good enough."

Like Terah, Abram's father—he started out for Canaan, but when he got to Harran, he called it quits (see Gen. 11:31).[1]

How dangerous, to set the brake and wedge a brick under each wheel. To imagine that we are already there, wherever that might be, initiates the slow snuffing out of the embers of our dreams. When we settle, we may stop searching for the next step in our growth journey toward learning, toward healing. Toward being a blessing. A plateau is a place to recover, not to park and plant a garden. It's a spot to catch our breath before we hit the next hill.

Plateaus are pleasant and necessary, and a campsite is essential. But either we break camp soon or we break our promise to push forward. Jesus said, "Follow me," not, "Camp out with me." At some point, we must blow the sand from the compass of our soul, shake out the creases in the map, and study our next move.

Time to get rolling. You know what they say, after all: move it or lose it. There are good reasons for wheels on a motor home.

TRAVELING MERCY
Dear one,
How I long to fuel the fire
Of your dreams,
To send sparks
Flying
Out into the world
From the adventure
That is your life.
Rest is good.
A permanent campsite,

Not so much.
So rest up,
Because there is much
Joy
Awaiting us
Together.
Blow off the sand
And pull up the pegs
And let's break camp.
Time to roll out.
People need what only you
Can offer.

NOTE TO SELF
Rest and revive to stay alive.

NOTE
1. There is some question about whether God called Abram from Ur or from Harran after he moved with Terah, but tradition and some manuscripts point to Ur.

MARCH 23

DESERT PLATEAU AND WAGONS HO!

> They set out.
> —Genesis 12:5

To keep the calling and the promise alive, Abram had to keep moving. No long-term plateaus allowed, no RV parking for extended stays. Some people consider plateaus as properties of the middle-aged set, those ripe for a midlife crisis. But a plateau isn't age or gender related. Plateau thinking sneaks up and attacks us from behind, an insidious invader of our mind and spirit.

One young woman, the bright star at her private school growing up, graduated from college and landed a position in a highly credentialed fine arts school as a music teacher. The job swallowed her soul's song with its extra demands. Her world turned gray. For most people, plateaus don't remain level for long, and hers slid downhill into depression.

Last summer, she set some boundaries and found a job in another district, one with more reasonable expectations. She is listening to the longing in her soul, which is to make the most of her music and audition for musicals. As life slowly seeps back in, her bounce is returning.

Another friend pursues growth consistently. As a medical doctor, she's aware of the connection between emotional health and physical wellbeing. She's taken courses on leadership for abuse survivors, spiritual disciplines, brain mapping, counseling training, and respite care for ministers. At each of these junctures, she'd plateaued and needed an injection of fresh focus and wisdom. More than that, she needed to have fresh blessing to give to the people she met and ministered to in both her practice and her daily life.

Not everyone has money or time to invest in new pursuits. But we can still enter the cycle of blessing, regardless of age or income or other demographic limitations. Unless you live in unincorporated areas, libraries are free. Book clubs abound. What about special courses at a local church? Classes at community colleges cover all the disciplines, and auditing is often free. These offer life-giving information but also critical human intersection and the opportunity to keep blessing.

What about volunteering at a senior residence if you're young or at a youth center if you're older? My mother-in-law at seventy-five is starting to teach computer skills to inmates at the county jail. She laughs and says, "They won't let me in with my crutch because it might be used as a weapon."

Take a risk. When have you said, "I've always wanted to . . ." or "I could *never* do that"? Well, do it! Find someone who has done it, enlist moral support, team up, and get going. Find places where you can give: tutoring, nurseries, homeless shelters, prisons, mowing a neighbor's lawn, mentoring. These places ensure that the blessing wheel continues to rotate. When we live out the promise, "You will be a blessing," we find that we are actually living in the promise: "I will bless you." Maybe it's time to "set out" just like Abram.

TRAVELING MERCY
Dear one,
To stop is crippling
To your song,
To your soul,
To the blessing.
So what gifts
Might you grow?
What mountains
Or hills might you climb?
What will you do
To set out
And keep rolling?
Because as long as there is breath
There is life.
So let's breathe
And really live,
Together.

NOTE TO SELF
Keep growing to keep giving.

MARCH 24

CANAANITES IN OUR PROMISED LAND

At that time the Canaanites were in the land.

—Genesis 12:6

Abram traveled hundreds of miles—maybe four hundred crow miles. Who knows how many hoof miles with every kind of terrain and a caravan. Like moving a small village, between all his stuff and the people in his life and the livestock without which no nomad could survive. All this based on the words of an invisible Being he'd never before heard from so directly. Talk about faith. He'd never seen this Being, though the longing for an encounter with deity, with a power outside of ourselves, seems to be a fairly universal hope.

And then, he reached the lands in Canaan where, surprise, there were Canaanites living. How, based on the revelation thus far, did Abram know to follow the route to Canaan, and how, based on the revelation thus far, did he also decide to stop? Who knows! But he walked forward, trusting.

But the Canaanites—what on earth were they doing in the land God promised to him? Had he heard correctly, to go? Was he truly listening to that inner sense, that still voice, which pressed a direction on him daily? If so, why this? Why now? Why Canaanites in *his* promised land?

Isn't that the way of it? We think we have this corner covered, that this is our turf and we have the rights to it. Wait, what are these people doing here messing up our lawn? People make our lives so complicated.

Do we really think we get to plant grass and then stick up a "Keep off the grass" sign? Or are we invited into a promised land with the express purpose of living out that promise to anyone who passes by and to the neighbors who have lived there for years and years—even if the neighbors were offspring of Noah's bad-boy son Ham, whose own son Canaan was cursed because of his father's actions (see Gen. 9:20–27)?

We might not like our neighbors. But God didn't promise us a deserted desert resort. God promised to lead us, and bless us, and make us a blessing.

So, have at it. Who are your Canaanites? How can you live among them and bless them without anesthetizing your faith and calling?

It's reassuring that right after the Scriptures tell us about the Canaanites in the Promised Land, they also tell us, "The LORD appeared to Abram" (Gen. 12:7).

May God appear to us as well. We just have to know that God takes on the guise of the stranger, the orphan, the widow, the homeless, the hungry, and the prisoner. Oh, and the Canaanite.

TRAVELING MERCY
Dear one,
Welcome to this (temporary) spot,
This place to call
Home,
At least for today.
Throw out the welcome mat,
But know this:
You are still a guest
In this land,
So live with respect
And love your neighbors
As yourself,
As I love you.
That should do it
Until it's time
To get a move on.

NOTE TO SELF
Live today by loving the strangers around me.

MARCH 25

THEN AGAIN

> The LORD appeared to Abram and said, "To your offspring I will give this land."
>
> —GENESIS 12:7

Abram took a gander at God's sweeping offer, but then a famine parched the forever-land. "Some plan this is," he thought, and off he headed to Egypt.

A famine in the land. Seriously? We think we have a handle on this plan, know just how God will define and dole out the blessings . . . and then a famine. A twist in our self-devised plotline and off we go in search of greener pasture. Doesn't that tell us right there that we trust the gift more than the Giver?

Part of the problem is that we expect the Giver to look a certain way, act a certain way, and have a gift in hand that we believe fits us perfectly. Never mind that we're often supposed to grow into our gifts. When the gift doesn't match our expectation, we not only refuse the gift, but also give up on the Giver. Haven't we left God's side sometimes because he didn't behave like we expected? Haven't we abandoned the padded seat in church because the promises preached didn't appear to line up with the promises received? Or because the answers didn't seem to work with our questions, like the multiple choice test got scrambled? Or because there were multiple possible answers for one question? Or maybe the questions didn't have answers and we prefer absolutes?

So off we stroll, looking for Egypt, looking for something that fits our definition of God's blessings as well as our timetable for their distribution. Where is your Egypt? What is your default setting when this day or moment or situation or relationship or life isn't what you expected? Where do you run when life is hard and God's promises seem vague or used up or a whole lot less than projected?

We head to our own south-of-the-border quick fix, like Abram heading for Egypt. But it turns out we're wreaking havoc on our lives and our loved ones' lives all while playing mini-god or with many gods, or simply dwindling away our lives.

But God was clear with Abram and the promise holds, no matter the feast or the famine. God is quite capable of hitting reset in ways we can't imagine to get us back home.

Wouldn't it be easier, however, on all of us, if we stopped to think through our plans first? Stopped to ask the question: What am I hoping for? What am I frightened of? What do I believe about God right now? Is God bigger than what I know or don't know about God? God surely knew a famine torched a path to Canaan, but he still said, "All the land that you see I will give to you and your offspring forever." The facts on earth—there is no food, the country is ravaged by famine, the world around us heaves in pain—didn't change the facts of God's faithfulness.

And just the same, our inability to see beyond the burnt-out ground in front of us doesn't change God's promise to us or

God's calling of us. We hold on to the promise, and hold onto God. Grass or no grass, God is good.

TRAVELING MERCY
Dear one,
How I long for you
To meet my gaze
And to see
That I love you,
That I offer you
Not just gifts,
But I offer you
Myself.
And of course,
Of course the grass grows
Wherever you aren't,
Or at least it looks like it does
From your view.
But I see the long view,
And I know how both famine and feast
Can grow your soul.
So don't walk away
Or run away
Or slip away
With me here
In the unknown.
And know this,
We'll be mowing
Before long.

NOTE TO SELF
Whether full or in famine, feast on God's faithfulness.

MARCH 26

DESERT BLESSING

> Now there was a famine in the land, and Abram went down
> to Egypt to live there for a while because the famine was severe.
>
> —Genesis 12:10

Deserts exist on every continent, swallowing 20 percent of the earth's land.[1] That's a lot of desert. There's a lot of desert in our personal journeys as well, maybe more than 20 percent, spiritually speaking. The desert is a common denominator, this perpetual assault of change, of problems and solution-seeking, and of trying to get through to the next day. And they will continue to companion us in this season and year of our Lord—the year that belongs to our Lord and not to us, not really, not at all. From Eden to Egypt we have all traveled, and our ongoing journey in desert places began with that exile, the exodus that changed everything. And deserts were the Israelites' common experience, too.

From the beginning, God led the Israelites, and the path often included sand. If we map the Israelites' paths with dotted lines, we end up with a super-highway of dots leading into and out of desert places. Even Israel, the land God promised to give Abram and his descendants, the Promised Land, is semiarid. It's quite desert in places and almost desert in others.

MARCH 26

Abram, called out of Ur into a great big promise, found himself in the middle of a severe famine. So off he headed to Egypt. This seems ironic when you look at pictures of Egypt and its sand and sun and lack of vegetation. Except for the region around the Nile, it doesn't appear to be a utopia of food resources and possibly wasn't on God's travel itinerary. But the Lord had a plan to provide for Abram and thus for all who would follow, those who would be the fulfillment of God's promise to Abram. The desert was an essential part of the itinerary. Deserts don't limit God's faithfulness and can in fact reveal that faithfulness.

Whether located in the Promised Land or outside of it, the desert must serve a purpose, if Abram landed there, because God promised that the whole earth would be blessed through him. Aren't we, by adoption, part of that spiritual lineage, the people God called and the people God leads? Then, somehow, there is a conversion that happens in the desert places.

Sometimes, at first, the desert brings out the worst in us, maybe just to show us that conversion is necessary. Abram's detour to Egypt, and his fear, placed his wife and his future family tree, in danger. But God refused to let fear have the final word on the passage to freedom.

The desert sorts out our sin and our sinful reactions, our fears and our fearful actions.

And that too is part of the blessing.

TRAVELING MERCY
Dear one,
Tip your chin to my face
And look at me, now.
No longer let your sin and pain
Drag you through your days.
Let me lead you.
If you will but trust me,
Your sin will not win.
Focus on my promise
Rather than your problems
That landed you in the desert.
If you watch,
You will see that I am leading you.
You will see.
This place of in-between
Really is part of the blessing.

NOTE TO SELF
Sin won't win, nor will the desert I'm in.

NOTE
1. National Geographic, "Deserts: Arid, but Full of Life," *National Geographic*, accessed June 13, 2014, http://environment.nationalgeographic.com/environment/habitats/desert-profile/.

MARCH 27

DESERT TIME

> I trust in you, LORD; I say, "You are my God."
> My times are in your hands.
>
> —PSALM 31:14–15

For the longest time, all my watches were broken. They'd split apart at the hinges of the band and face, or the battery was dead, or the face had cracked, or the second hand spun freely. During those days, my watch was my cell phone, and I punched it to check the time. Sometimes I am in three different time zones in three days, and when I look at my watch, I haven't the faintest idea what time it really is. I'll glance at my wrist in Pennsylvania and realize I'm on Pacific time, or in Indiana and my watch registers mountain time.

In the desert, it's easy to lose track of time. Hours and days blend together in a haze of heat or cold, and the nights roll endlessly past. Some days, the desert feels like a prison, but there are no walls on which to make chicken scratches of each day that passes.

And those unending days and nights can drag us down into despair, into a restless impatience to find the way out; to put an end to the aimless wandering, to settle up accounts, to get a plan, and to get moving forward. We think. But that isn't really possible, because in the desert, we live in a different kind of time zone, measured by God alone. Desert time. God time.

The God who lives outside of time sees us, knows us by name, and is aware of the pain of living in desert places. God knows; God has a plan. It rarely looks like a plan we'd have hatched ourselves, with timetables and ETAs at the other side of the desert. On our itinerary, the ferry is waiting at our final destination to carry us across the river. Until then, on God's itinerary, the destination may not even be a physical place. We no longer live in a time zone. We live in a timeless zone.

Plus, our journey is not like our neighbor's. We compare travelogs and feel short-changed or unloved or abandoned, if our routes differ. Maybe their house sold as soon as they pounded the stake in the soil, and off they went; you're two years and counting. Maybe their unemployment season lasted only a week or two, or never, and you have spent months or years in the desert of job loss and job search. Or their health issues were resolved, or their wanderer returned home a new person, or their marriage healed in a miraculous turn of events.

But that's their desert schedule, their timetable. Not yours or mine. Our desert time will be crafted for each of us, though not necessarily designed to lead us to a solution to our problems. Rather, to lead us to God's heart and to our own heart.

How God specifically works or worked in other people's lives is not our measure. The fact *that* God worked in others' lives *is* our measure. This is the same God; ours is the same travel agent. This is the God who leads us, the God whose desert time is always the right time, even if our watches read differently.

I glance at my watch. I seem to be wearing it upside down today. Maybe that's OK, for this day in the desert time zone.

TRAVELING MERCY
Dear one,
Beloved,
Your watch is upside down
In the desert.
Just watch me
Instead of your neighbors and fellow sojourners,
And trust my timetable.
Sync your watch with my
Eternal clock.
Put away your efficiency charts
And your frequent flyer polls
And decide
Today
That time
Is on your side.

NOTE TO SELF
Today, I'm setting my watch to God's time zone.

MARCH 28

DECEIT IN THE DESERT

> You are [Sarah's] daughters if you do
> what is right and do not give way to fear.
>
> —1 Peter 3:6

Sooner or later, it sure seems like the wilderness will bring out the worst in us. Abram had logged a lot of steps on his pedometer when that famine enticed him to Egypt. Along the way, he glanced at his stunning wife, Sarai, and pulled her aside before they entered yet another desert. "Quick," he said. "Tell them you're my sister. Otherwise they'll take my life, thinking you're my wife" (see Gen. 12:10–20).

Abram, still wrestling with fear, wasn't thinking beyond his own fate. Fear can make us narrow-minded. He handed his beloved over to the king. How did Sarai feel about this betrayal? The king took her to be his wife—do you shudder to think of that?—compounding the cost of Abram's deceit.

The Scriptures remain silent about Sarai's reaction to all this treachery, to the scars that likely resulted from the illicit relationship Abram's fear forced her into. But couldn't she speak up? Not without making her husband out to be a liar or a half-liar or a scoundrel (or all of the above), and endangering his life and perhaps her own. Not in a society where women were tools or chattel, or both.

What a way to wrack and ruin a relationship. Maybe that's your story, whether married or single. That experience of betrayal and of helplessness . . . Maybe you're in the desert because someone abandoned you, like Abram abandoned Sarai. A precious relationship has been crippled by defection—yours, or another's. Maybe not even defection. Maybe the crippling has come gradually, by neglect or the grinding away of trust, of missed connections, of lack of effort, of boredom. But the end result? It's betrayal.

Betrayal happens in Christian marriages about as often as in the general society. Maybe the betrayal looks like workaholism, or an addiction to sports, shopping, food, friends, pornography, romance novels, alcohol, or volunteerism. Maybe betrayal looks like a refusal to grow or to invest in or to commit to the relationship. Or just letting love grow cold through neglect and passivity.

Even though Abram didn't speak up for his wife, God did. God inflicted all manner of serious diseases on Pharaoh and his household because of Sarai. The king of Egypt returned her to Abram, fuming, and sent him packing. "Why didn't you tell me she was your wife? Why did you say, 'She is my sister,' so I took her to be my wife?" (Gen. 12:18–19).

Another's defection isn't for us to belabor. Rather, we heal by understanding our own reaction or response and God's response toward us. For Sarai to heal from such betrayal couldn't have been easy, to saddle up again beside this man who in cowardice gave her over to be used by the king. I can only imagine the angry conversations and the cold shoulders after their reunion. It makes sense, doesn't it, that it took much journeying for her to be ready to conceive? Ultimately, she stayed the course and "did not give way to fear" (see 1 Pet. 3:6). She came through the desert and is listed in Hebrews 11:11 as a woman of faith.

Abram feared. But Sarai chose differently. She chose to forgive.

The desert provides a good sorting-out place. The wide-open spaces beg us to reconsider, to reinvest. To resist our fear and hang on to the promise. This is the route to freedom.

TRAVELING MERCY
Dear one,
I know it's hard
And that your fear is heavy,
And the possibility of betrayal
And of abandonment
In the desert
Abandonment as huge as
The desert itself.
Of course people will betray you.
But I am your God.
I will not abandon you,
Nor will I ever betray you.
You are my heir.
I have made a promise to you,
Even when others break theirs.
Cling to me.
Register your wounds and fears in my ledger
Then resist your fears.

It's not easy,
But it's the best way through
This deep darkness.
I'm loving you every step of the way.

NOTE TO SELF
Fear and abandonment can lead me to God's faithfulness.

MARCH 29

I STAND CORRECTED

So Pharaoh summoned Abram.
—Genesis 12:18

Abram entered Egypt with legitimate qualms. A nomad crossing the border into the wealthy and progressive country, a place long settled, looking for favor? Of course he felt terrified, which explains (but doesn't justify) why he threw his wife Sarai under the bus when he said, "Quick, pretend to be my sister, so Pharaoh doesn't kill me on account of you."

After all manner of disease broke loose on Pharaoh's household, Pharaoh, a wise man, immediately seized on the cause and the effect: Abram had lied about the beautiful woman, Pharaoh had then taken her to be his wife, and the fury of heaven resulted in disease. God stirred up chaos within the kingdom to protect the line about to be established. And Pharaoh, the worldly and wise leader of the Egyptian empire, called Abram on the carpet.

No, Pharaoh berated the immigrant for his lies and booted him out of the castle and the country.

Chastisement doesn't always come from a godly source, and isn't it sometimes hard to listen to someone outside the flock confront our shoddy ethics? But that renders the criticism no less valid. Perhaps it is even more valid, because people who don't deal in grace but rather have a business to run and a bottom line to protect are less afraid to tell us the truth. Just because it didn't seem to come straight from God doesn't mean God didn't send the discipline by another's hand and voice.

This doesn't mean we hear it easily. We can moan "Unfair!" and "Where's the love?" but we are not exceptions to the call to high conduct, and we sure aren't exceptional. Abram might have been the projected head of a long and lasting family that would grow exponentially to bless the entire world, and God clearly called him. But just as clearly, God called him on the carpet to behave like a blessed man who blessed others (including his wife).

Even so, mercifully, Abram escaped with his wife and people, a man made rich by straying into Egypt. The Scriptures tell us that Pharaoh "treated [him] well for her sake" (Gen. 12:16), a fabulous commentary on Sarai's actions, and gave Abram servants, sheep, cattle, donkeys, and even camels. Abram may have been the only one to profit immediately, and only time would tell about the impact of this trip to Egypt—detour or destination? We'll see. But what we know for sure is that God protected him and Sarai, in spite of unwise decisions, and Abram continued on the journey to wisdom.

May it be so for us as well. May we process our failures, and proceed forward. Richer from the travel.

TRAVELING MERCY
Dear one,
That's what I want for you—
Richer for the travel.
Richer in wisdom.
Richer in grace.
Richer in repentance.
Richer.
Knowing my hand
Both leads and corrects
And draws and connects
The dots between who you are
And who you will be.
And one day it will all make sense.
You'll see.
Meanwhile,
Live up
To your call.

NOTE TO SELF
Grace and growth are not mutually exclusive.
Choose both.

MARCH 30

YOU-TURN

> From the Negev he went from place to place until
> he came to Bethel, to the place between Bethel and Ai
> where his tent had been earlier and where he had first
> built an altar. There Abram called on the name of the Lord.
>
> —Genesis 13:3–4

How significant that after the debacle in Egypt, Abram left with great riches and his wife—listed here in reverse order of importance if he was going to hold on to God's promise for him—virtually unscathed. Except, of course, what this might have done to his already fragile marriage, given years of disappointment due to childlessness. And except, of course, when our own excursions into Egypt delay God's destination for us.

After being reprimanded by possibly the most powerful man on the continent, likely the person of the year on the cover of *Time* magazine in that era, Abram plodded straight back to the altar he'd built in Bethel, the place where, we are told, he first "called on the name of the Lord" (Gen. 12:8).

This might be one of the smartest acts so far in his nomadic life. After being a tad off-center during the entire flight to Egypt, he returned to the place he knew, the place where he'd first called on this God, this place commemorated by an altar.

There Abram "called on the name of the LORD" (Gen. 13:4).

At this point, don't you release your breath a little? Doesn't your chest loosen with relief? Maybe Abram was learning from his folly, maybe there was hope for him after all. Rather than let failure sideswipe him and his faith, in order to get clear again he returned to the God who called him. He called on the name of the Lord.

Failure. The great inevitable for anyone with a heartbeat. But how to handle it? Assume the worst about yourself and the best about God, really. Assume that without God's help and hand, we are the worst sinners. But don't stop there. Assume the best about God: that God is bigger than our detours, that God's goodness trumps our idiocy. That God's favor never ends.

And favor, just to recap, isn't based on our merits. Not now, not then, not ever. Favor—blessing—is based entirely on God's goodness, on God's love toward us regardless of our disastrous attempts at and attacks on life. No prison bars can block God's favor: neither prison bars made of iron and steel and lock and key, nor prison bars constructed of shame and failure and poor showings in the public opinion polls and in the privacy of our own tents.

Abram had every reason to be ashamed, to skulk off the trail and never return. But he didn't listen to his own shame. He remembered two critical realities: God's calling and God's promise. Those two things do not change.

And he headed back to where he'd first called on the Lord.

We can do that, too. Face our failure head-on and then hurry straight to God, to the place where we call on the Lord. It's a U-turn and a you-turn.

TRAVELING MERCY
Dear one,
Failure is part of the plan
To turn you back,
To turn you around,
To lead you into
A new place,
A greener place
Of faith
And of grace.
The sooner you turn
In your pain
And call on me,
The quicker the gain.
So come back.
Make the call.
I'm here.
Always.

NOTE TO SELF
Never too late for a you-turn toward grace.

MARCH 31

THE BIGNESS OF THE BLESSING

So Abram said to Lot, "Let's not have any quarreling between you
and me, or between your herders and mine, for we are close relatives."

—Genesis 13:8

After his brush with his own humanity and a dressing down by a world power, Abram returned to Canaan, returned to God, and then turned to Lot. Even as Abram's possessions increased in Egypt—he left ranking high on the Fortune 500 list—so did Lot's. The blessing began to permeate the edges and boundaries of the lives of people around Abram.

But as goods increase, so does the maintenance of those goods . . . and also trouble. Sure enough, there wasn't enough land for the cattle and sheep and whatever other straggling livestock they'd accumulated. Not enough grazing pastures and not enough water to support the animals, let alone the people keeping company with Lot and Abram.

And then turf wars erupted between the various herders in the camps. Sides were drawn over the maintenance of the blessings. Isn't that something? Our blessings rise up and fight among themselves.

But Abram began a new season of wisdom, it seems, on his return and his turning. He surveyed the land and then fixed his attention on Lot. "Let's not have any quarreling," he said. "Not between the two of us, nor between our herdsmen. We are relatives," he said.

And herein lies the lesson. May our possessions never ever separate us from our loved ones or cause dissension between us. You may laugh and say, "What possessions?" but the moment our possessions (or standard of living, or desire for acquisition or power or a great name, or any other want that attracts our heart) outweigh the human beings standing in our circle—or outside our circle—we begin to live unbalanced lives. Our possessions start to possess us, and to marginalize people. We can't let the family silver separate us from the people eating with the forks and spoons.

Family feud, anyone? Heard any great stories about the reading of wills lately where the survivors descend into baseness as they claw for what they believe they deserve? And who deserves anything left behind when loved ones vacate their bodies and evacuate to the ultimate promised land? We earned none of it, and we deserve none of it. God's blessings are not our right. They are a privilege. Anything that remains is pure undeserved grace. But still, fights emerge.

Not so with Abram. There on the hills of Canaan, he recognized the problem and addressed its heart. Not the possessions, but the relationship: Let's not have any quarrels, for we are relatives.

And aren't we all relatives? Aren't we all related by the common ancestry of Adam and Eve, and now, for those of us who believe, in Christ? And isn't quarreling ultimately selfishness, an assertion of our rights over someone else's? But that doesn't really strike at the core, does it? The truth is deeper: quarreling is not just a sign of our weakness. It is a sign of our longings—to be safe and to be loved.

And in God's care, we are safe. And we are loved. Now we get to live like it. "Let's not have any quarreling between you and me . . . for we are relatives."

TRAVELING MERCY
Dear one,
All that you have
Is happily from my hand.
So yes, absolutely
Enjoy.
But also
Share.
Be gracious and generous.
Bless as I've blessed you.
That will be the end
Of any quarrels
When it comes to possessions,
Because it is all gift.
Mine to you,
Yours to others.
And you show others
My heart
When you live
As relatives
With no quarreling
Separating you.
So live on
And give on.

NOTE TO SELF
Today I'll live and give from God's blessings.

APRIL DEVOTIONS

APRIL 1

LOT IN LIFE

> Lot looked around and saw that the whole plain of the
> Jordan toward Zoar was well watered, like the
> garden of the LORD, like the land of Egypt.
>
> —GENESIS 13:10

Abram surveyed the land, looking past the crowded pastures and the red-faced, fed-up herdsmen, and said, "Is not the whole land before you? Let's part company. If you go to the left, I'll go to the right; if you go to the right, I'll go to the left" (Gen. 13:9).

We don't know how the land looked so soon after a famine. There's no word about whether the famine's devastation reversed while Abram and family holidayed in Egypt, or even how long they lived there before Pharaoh figured out the ruse. But the man who would father a nation, a nation that would ultimately bless the world, hightailed it out of Egypt with his wife and everything he owned, along with his nephew Lot.

Lot always leaves me with a sour taste in my mouth, like a shoddy, shambling relative of a celebrity who makes the news repeatedly because of bad behavior. But, because people's behavior only makes complete sense when we know their story, it's smarter to not judge. Maybe I would be even more of a disaster than Lot appeared to be. But my thoughts run away with me.

What to even say about Lot? Orphaned at an unknown age when his father died, he traveled with Grandpa Terah and all the aunts and uncles and any cousins he might have had and hauled off to Harran (which is, coincidently, also his deceased father's name). Immediately, relocation compounded his grief. It opened up multiple abandonment issue opportunities. So Abram draped an arm around Lot's shoulder and took him under his own wing of protection. Orphaned boy, childless man. It seemed a match made in heaven.

Lot traveled with Abram all those months and even years, and who knows what interesting vices the nephew accumulated in Egypt. But still, Abram deferred to him at this juncture: "You go first. You get the first pick of the land."

So Lot eyeballed the surroundings and decided on the richest, greenest, lushest area. Who can blame him? Any farmer with a brain would choose the area most likely to grow crops and support animals. The hugeness of Abram's faith sprouts from the pages. He nodded, looked again at his less lush, less green, less happy land and agreed. His faith exceeded the fields before him. He believed God was bigger than the poor soil and the burned-out grasses. Abram did more than make do. He kept turning his face to God and trusting God's panoramic view of the future rather than his own.

Regardless of the land we've been given—whether it is literal acreage or one room over someone's garage; whether land for us means our job, our family, or our possessions, paltry though they be—God's promise for Abram holds for us, as well: "I will bless you and make you a blessing, and all the peoples on earth will be blessed." We are part of that blessing, not a trickle-down effect that feels like a bit of humidity on a sauna-hot day, but rather the very real waterfall of God raining down forgiveness and grace from heaven. A new start every day.

Lot ran off to settle his land, but never learned to live in the blessing.

Abram, though? Abram turned to, and turned into, God's shoulder, and together they hoed the rows before them.

Even if our land doesn't look as green as our neighbor's, God has a green thumb. May we, like Abram, possess a faith bigger than the facts. A faith that outlives the brown fields and the famine. A faith big enough to grow and to bless others.

TRAVELING MERCY
Dear one,
Faith bigger than the facts.
That's a mouthful for today.
Bigger than the acts
Of another's selfishness,
The outworking of their wounds,
Which could in turn
Wound you.
But keep turning the soil
Of your own soul,
And you'll be the one
Coming up green and lush
And ripe with my presence.
It's the growing season.

NOTE TO SELF
I will hoe the rows, and God will provide the grow.

APRIL 2

LOOK AROUND YOU

"Go, walk through the length and breadth of the land."
—Genesis 13:17

The earth inches closer to the sun, and the snows covering our yard disappear below the surface of the long-hidden ground. If we had ears to hear, we would hear a quickening throughout the earth, a crackling into life of plants and living beings long asleep. The slow sloughing breath of hibernation hastens into the labored breathing of birth, of the crowning of life from the dark womb of earth.

For the earth utters breathy promises in the spring. The wind changes, blowing in hope from the south, nudging trees and grass into wakefulness. Expectation scents the air. The covenant of renewal rewrites itself with fresh ink that wets the page of every new day. A covenant of life being readied, of promised beauty yet to bud. Spring is a resurrection, when all we thought dead returns. The acorns sprout, and the maple spinners morph into seedlings. The bulb awakens and stretches stubby green arms from its resting place in the deep, cold dirt.

Winter-hardened soil converts into life-giving mud. The ground warms. Worms begin their travel season. Birds cock their heads, listening for subterranean movement, and ready themselves for feasting and creating the next generation. For their nests, they gather twigs and fluff and stray bits of the world.

Regardless of how much death happens in our lives—and can't you tick off some of the deaths of recent months on your fingers?—God built resurrection into the cycle of our year. Last year's leaves become this year's mulch, the living things that hibernate awaken and life returns. Sap opens the closed veins and courses again to the fingertips of the trees, dressing them in courage. Spring makes life livable, and believable.

After the triple disaster of earthquake, tsunami, and nuclear radioactivity in Japan in March 2011, as the world rallied to the aid of the distressed nation, the able-bodied people around that devastated country took in the homeless, fed the hungry, and searched rubble for survivors. In the midst of the ruin and shock, the cherry trees burst into life, their pink blossoms offering bouquets of hope to the grieving people. The trees bore valiant witness of a determined joy, a relentless life course.

Spring will come. Inward and outward. Irresistible hope stands on the doorstep of our souls, a suitor knocking, knocking. And we open the door, and there stands God, waiting on the stoop. "Will you come out and play, today? Come, see what I have done."

Listen to what God says next. "See what I have done. Just for you." And then, "Welcome back. Welcome back to life." We step over the threshold and into transformation. The world's. And our own.

TRAVELING MERCY

Dear one,
Take a breath.
Do you taste it in the air?
Life,
Hope,
New dreams,
The bulbs of resurrection
Reaching into the death
Of these past months
And years.
The world groans
For the new life.
And here it is
Every day,
The damp dew
Of grace and mercy,
Sunrise for your soul.
Will you wake up,
And breathe deeply,
And notice
This is your day,
The world's day?
New life.
Right now.
Spring thawing.

NOTE TO SELF
Yesterday's death won't derail today's life.

APRIL 3

NEVER QUITE HOME

*A man who had escaped came and reported
this to Abram the Hebrew.*

—Genesis 14:13

Abram is first called a Hebrew in Genesis 14:13, when a war refugee ran to find "Abram the Hebrew" to tell him of Lot's capture in the battle of the kings. Some concordances indicate that the word *Hebrew* is untranslated. But there is a possibility that the word meant "crossing," someone who crosses over. Crosses over a border or a river. Crosses over into a country. Crosses the line. It may be a general term for an exile or an alien. Abram the alien. Abram the exile. Abram, the one constantly crossing. And his life trek crisscrossed over the continent, from Ur to Harran, to Canaan and throughout that land, to Egypt, and back and forth.

Not only would this name, Hebrew, cling to Abram's life, but when he became the father of many nations, the entire people would be called Hebrews—crossing people, aliens, exiles. Foreigners. People without a homeland. Indeed, the people would live up to their name for many generations to follow. In the New Testament, the book of Hebrews—the book of the people who crossed over, the aliens, the exiles—tells us that the nation's early heroes died without ever reaching their homeland, but were seeking, always, the home yet to come.

"All these people were still living by faith when they died. They did not receive the things promised; they only saw them and welcomed them from a distance, admitting that they were foreigners and strangers on earth" (Heb. 11:13).

Foreigners and strangers on earth. Isn't that our lot in life, too? We don't fit in, not really, not with the people climbing corporate or social ladders, and not with the neighbors, and not with so many people in the world, because we (hopefully) live life to a different beat. Hopefully we live motivated, asking the right question. Not like Lot, who asked, "Is this profitable?" but rather, "Is this right?" Instead of seeking to profit, we seek to serve. We live the life of people who are crossing over—crossing over from this world to the next, crossing over from the journey to and from work and the grocery store and school and church, from the temporary daily world—into the world that will last forever. Like Abram, we seek that world yet to come. And unless our Messiah returns soon, we will die without receiving the things promised.

But in an amazing juxtaposition of life and Life, we end up receiving everything promised . . . on the other side.

So while we keep walking, we keep watching. Alien? Exile? One day we will have a homeland. And meanwhile, may we recognize the aliens among us, those in exile, and welcome them into the family.

It's a little like walking into a homeless shelter to help and realizing your kinfolk are all there on the sleeping pads in front of you, waiting and hoping, their eyes haunted with pain and with . . . something else. And that, in fact, you do not have a home either. So you take your seat with your family and turn your eyes toward heaven, the unmistakable pressure of chain-link longing twining about your chest.

The longing for a home yet to be.

May God allow us to be "Hebrews," strangers and exiles, always crossing over, and always, always reaching out to the stranger and exile among us.

TRAVELING MERCY
Dear one,
Sometimes you ache
For the home yet to be.
For the times when you are the stranger,
The foreigner,
The exile,
The one always waiting
For what you do not receive,
Know this:
You do not wait in vain.
And while you wait,
May your longing for home
Help you welcome others
Into the home that is your life
And your kindness.
One day we will all be home together.
No longer foreigners,
No longer crossing-over people.
Children of heaven.
Home.

NOTE TO SELF
Let homelessness lead me to God and others.

APRIL 4

A PLACE NAMED PEACE

"Praise be to God Most High."
—Genesis 14:20

In the middle of Abram's lifeline, a bunch of kings battled over turf rights. Four kings duked it out with five other kings, and the underdogs won, capturing the locals, the loot, and Lot to boot. Abram entered the fray when he learned of Lot's capture, surprising the armies with a military move unknown at that time. He recovered all the stolen goods and the prisoners of war.

To the victor go the spoils. Abram, a non-king, could have fashioned his own crown and declared himself king of the territory. Remember way back when Abram let Lot have the best land? When Lot's eyes got bigger than his ethics? He landed in a heap of trouble, becoming a POW. Now Abram rescued him and emerged the victor. All over again, Abram could have had that plot of land—interesting turn of events.

Talk about a redirect. But Abram managed to maintain focus on the real promise. He didn't embark on an ego mission, settling into a role he designed for himself. God hadn't promised that another nation or king would make Abram rich.

God promised to bless him. So Abram refused the spoils of war and sought God's blessing, not the king of Sodom's. Here we see his true heart.

Not only did he show military and relational wisdom, but Abram maintained perspective by holding God's promise in the forefront of his faith. God promised to make of Abram a great nation, and doesn't greatness come from helping others? Not by beating a bunch of local gangs. God promised a nation bigger than human hands and military prowess could create. Abram hadn't entered the fray for the spoils; he'd fought for his nephew Lot and kept trekking after the promise.

And because Abram followed God's lead, he could say no to King Sodom's offer of spoils. He knew his life promise wasn't an earthly crown but a long line of footsteps trailing after God.

But another king also met him in the King's Valley with gifts of bread and wine. "Blessed be Abram by God Most High," Melchizedek greeted him, "and praise be to God Most High." Melchizedek, whose name meant "king of righteousness," was king of a place named Peace. He is the first priest to appear in the Scriptures and foreshadows the One who would come many years later, the Prince of Peace and the King of Kings.

King Sodom offered the temptation of war spoils, but Melchizedek hinted at the peace and righteousness yet to come, the ultimate promise of God who would rescue us from all our battles and ultimately win the war.

And don't we all, fresh from battle and fighting, come to people to remember God's faithfulness and offer them the gifts of bread and wine, of food and sustenance, the gift of blessing? Don't we turn our eyes to heaven, unimpressed by another's riches but aware of the huge costs of their battles and their valor in fighting, and bless God and bless the warriors among us?

And are we not all warriors in some fashion, fighting against the temptations of this world and fighting to keep our focus on the One who promises to bless us and make us a blessing?

Don't we all struggle to fight the good fight of faith, to battle against our own specific temptations, and to live into the reign of the Prince of Peace and the King of Kings?

It's easy to get confused by our wants and our needs, and not realize that what we really want is God's blessing over us.

Holding fast to the promise, we begin to live in a place named Peace.

TRAVELING MERCY
Dear one,
Yes to the victor go the spoils;
And the spoils of battle
Are renewed faith
And a fighting weight
That outlasts
The mightiest opponent.
Because you are strong?
No, because I am
God Most High,
Creator of heaven and earth,
And I am
The one who delivers,
The one who leads.
So fix your focus on me,

On my promises,
And live toward
The place of peace.
It is worth the battle.
And know this:
I have already
Won the war.

NOTE TO SELF
Fight the right fight today.
And bless warriors along the way.

APRIL 5

DESERT FEAR

> "Do not be afraid, Abram. I am your shield,
> your very great reward."
>
> —Genesis 15:1

Fear. What a simple, yet complicated reaction to the desert, to the calling of the desert. And what a common reaction, for that matter. No wonder Abram felt fear; no wonder we do. And no wonder we circle around fear for much of our lives. We have certain promises from God but years go by, and we are not certain, or we are less and less certain, that those promises are ever going to be fulfilled.

Abram was afraid. Though he'd accumulated great wealth en route, following God's direction into all the unknowns, the future was anything but secure. He didn't know from one day to the next what would happen. He and his 318 trained men had just won a major battle against four kings, winning back his nephew Lot and all of Lot's extended family and possessions. He'd won the battle, but what was the war, and how might he fare in that? I doubt he expected such a fight in the desert. And I doubt, too, that he expected that the journey to "where I will show you," as God said in the beginning, was going to be so long and so laborious.

We feel fear, as well. We don't have the foggiest notion when our prayers for deliverance will be answered, when we will arrive at the promised land. We don't even know, perhaps, what that promised land is. Nor could we imagine the skirmishes encountered in the traveling, the disappointments and discouragements. Besides that, we don't know how the circumstances will end, or maybe even if they will end. Whether our problems will be solved or remain to torment us for the rest of our lives. We have no guarantees on this frightening trek.

But that's not really true, is it? Maybe we do have a guarantee, for God's promise to Abram holds for us, as well. "Don't be afraid," God said, "for I am your shield, your very great reward." After the mighty battle just passed through, maybe Abram at his ripe age wasn't sure he could endure another, wasn't sure he could even lift his own shield one more time.

Sometimes in the wilderness I have felt the same. I didn't think I could withstand one more problem, one more fight, one more surprising unknown. As much as I like surprises, these were not the surprises of my dreams. Too often they felt like nightmares, these encounters with my own insufficiency and lack of wisdom and total bankruptcy of emotional and physical energy. These run-ins with my internal enemy of fear demoralized me and hurt people I love.

But God made a promise, and we can hold onto that promise: "I am your shield." God is our shield. God is the barrier between us and our problems, us and the desert, us and the painful uncertainty so rife in the desert places. If God is our shield, then the shield will stand against the onslaught of the enemy.

Besides, consider all the other resourceful uses of the shield—a covering in the night, a hat in the heat, a trough for water, a barrier from the wind and blowing sands, or even a pan to hold over the fire and cook meat. God is our shield, covering us in the night, barricading us from the wind and the sand, providing for us in immensely creative ways.

No doubt our fear, and the fallout from our fear, will rise up again and again in our personal unknowns. When they do, we can envision our God as our shield, the one who comes between us and the elements and who absorbs the blows of the wilderness. We can take our fears to God and then crouch behind that shield. We can remind ourselves and God of the truth: "You are our shield."

TRAVELING MERCY
Dear one,
Of course you are afraid.
Fear may be a natural reaction,
Because you don't know the future
Here in your barren places.
But I stand between you and your future,
Between you and your fears.
List those fears, and then lift them to me.
I promise that I will be your shield
In every single battle,
In every storm,
In every difficulty.
Do not be afraid,
For I am your shield.

NOTE TO SELF
God's shield can separate me from my fear.

APRIL 6

DESERT DESIRE

"Your very great reward."
—Genesis 15:1

When God told Abram not to be afraid, that God was Abram's very great reward, was God answering a question that Abram wasn't asking? "Don't be afraid. I'm your great reward." I don't see Abram asking God about any reward. It seems as though Abram was less anxious about collecting goods than about collecting on God's promise—after all, what more could he need? He'd become a very rich man on his sojourn. Well, maybe there was one thing missing. Descendants to outnumber the sand. Abram certainly saw a lot of sand. So in the wind and rain and dark of night, Abram looked around him and remembered God's promise. The promise that was unfulfilled.

God promised to be a shield, to be Abram's reward, and Abram came back with, "But you promised. What about my babies? I'm going to have my butler be my heir, at this rate. What about all those offspring?"

This man had everything by the world's standards, then and now. Except he didn't have his heart's desire—a child.

And maybe your heart's desire is missing, too. You've trusted God all this way, all these days, and never wavered from the seemingly wayward leading in the wilderness, your heart's desire ever before you. And though your life has much to show for the trip, there's a part of your soul, a teeny part perhaps, that holds a mustard seed of disappointment or despair.

You've trusted God in the wilds, and still, no answer to that heart's desire. While waiting for freedom to ring, you've memorized the Scriptures about trusting in the Lord with all your heart and receiving your heart's desire as a result, and still . . . no heart's desire on the vast horizon. Nothing to show for all your trusting. Isn't that a raw deal? Doesn't that feel like a false promise, a real rip-off?

The danger of that mustard seed of disappointment is that it will grow and become a huge flowering tree full of bitter fruit, with deep roots that reach clear into the caverns of your heart. It can take over your entire soul, this bitterness. And that's a real danger. The other danger is that because we haven't found our heart's desire, we end up not desiring, not dreaming at all. We suffocate that dream because it hurts to dream.

Maybe God is saying, to Abram, to you, to me: "I want to be your very great reward. I want to be enough for you. I want to be your all-in-all. I want you to desire me above all the gifts I could give you or have already given you. I want you, I have chosen you, I have called you into this place so that I can be your security, I can be your dream. I can be yours. And you can be mine."

I consider this. It has been a long hike, disappointing in many ways. I wonder if you, too, can list your disappointments, the ways your desires seem to be thwarted? I realize, rather than any collectibles, I want to collect on this promise: that God will be my very great reward. And so I bring my desires, my heart's great desires, to God's feet. I want God; to live without him is to live in the midst of death. Whether or not my desires are ever fulfilled, I want God. And maybe that's the whole point of the journey. Maybe that's the secret to freedom.

TRAVELING MERCY
Dear one,
I know you are disappointed.
On this journey into the wilderness,
Your soul filled with distress,
And sometimes you're ready to give up
On those dreams.
I want to hear your heart's desires
Right now.
Can you tell me, again?
I haven't led you willy-nilly into this
Desert place.
Nor will I ever leave you here,
Alone, abandoned, orphaned.
Bring your desires to me,
And let me convert them, redirect them,
So that whatever happens,
You will have your reward.
You will have
My presence,
My love,
My promise.
I promise.

NOTE TO SELF
If God is my heart's desire,
then I have my very great reward.

APRIL 7

THE REAL REWARD

"Sovereign LORD, what can you give me since I remain childless?"
—GENESIS 15:2

After Abram's victory over the kings, he could have been flushed with pride and power. He could have succumbed to lust or a power trip when the king of Sodom offered the spoils of battle. But the not-yet patriarch refused those detours.

And then God reappeared to him in a vision and promised, "I'm your shield. Your reward will be grand!" (Gen. 15:1 MSG). In fact, God's promises and presence bracket the entire episode of Abram running around like a young warrior.

What could God possibly give Abram to substitute for his biggest desire, the promised child? "I'm not worried about rewards," Abram implied. He answered God's reassurance with striking honesty and practicality. His honesty allowed him to voice his doubt. He redirected the conversation to his main point, his big longing: "Look, God. I want the child you promised me. But, since you aren't delivering, I will handle it. After all, I'm a wealthy man and without an heir, so who will benefit from my wealth? I have to get cracking and fix this problem."

"What else can I do?" Abram scuffed his sandal in the sand and shrugged his shoulders. "I'll just make my servant my heir." Sure wasn't what Abram expected when God unveiled the glorious family portrait, with a family more than the grains of sand in the desert. Which is considerable, when you think about it. And Abram surely had his gaze on the hourglass of his life, with its once-endless sands trickling away.

So Abram was ready to settle right then and adopt his trusted servant. Ironically, his servant's name was Eliezer. "God is my helper." You'd think that Abram would recognize what he was about to do: decide on the timing on his own and designate his servant as heir. His servant whose very name should have reminded Abram that God is his helper, too.

But we forget. We forget our name, we forget the names of the people in our lives who are meant to help us, and instead we think we will use them or substitute them for God's promises. It's tempting to just do it ourselves rather than to do the work of trust and submission to another's timing.

Even when we forget, God remembers the promises.

"This man will not be your heir, but a son who is your own flesh and blood will be your heir" (Gen. 15:4). And the image, day after night after year after decade while Abram waited and tried to trust?

"Look up at the heavens and count the stars . . ."

In the deep dark of night—and who of us has not experienced the deep dark?—we do just like Abram. Slip out through the tent flap into the night air crisp and cold, and look at the sky. And at the sign through the ages leading all the way to the Star of David, the bright Morning Star: the stars radiant in the night, opening the heavens, piercing the darkness.

Abram looked up, away from his darkness, into the brilliant night sky, and "believed the LORD, and he credited it to him as righteousness" (Gen. 15:6).

God credited Abram with righteousness, and Abram credited God with being righteous. Abram deserved nothing, but God put him at rights. In a remarkable early entry into the journals of grace, we glimpse the very beginning of the truth of the gospel that Christ lived and Paul taught: by grace are we saved, by faith. Not by law or by works, lest we should boast, but entirely because God reached out from heaven and specifically invited us into a relationship.

How do we know for sure? Go ahead. Take a gander at the stars tonight.

TRAVELING MERCY

Dear one,
Of course you have doubts,
And of course you try
To fix things yourself.
But let me
Put you aright.
Look outside.
I am the first sky-writer,
And have written my promise
For you to see.
It's too soon to settle,
So as long as you have breath
Look at the stars.
See if you can count them,
And know this: I can.

I flung them into place.
Remember that
When you doubt.
I will bring
My goodness to pass in your life.
Just look up.

NOTE TO SELF
Doubt is inevitable, but God's promise
outshines the dark.

APRIL 8

BUT THE LIGHT IS COMING

Thick and dreadful darkness came over him.
—Genesis 15:12

Abram fell into a deep sleep as the sun slipped below the western horizon. He'd spent the day preparing sacrifices for the ceremonial covenant God instituted. He'd swatted away the vultures from the carcasses, but at sunset, sleep claimed him.

And in the sleep, "thick and dreadful darkness came over him." Not just darkness, as in, it's night but the moon is outside and the stars too. No, try instead, brooding, evil, a place that feels like annihilation. A place of darkness so thick it would describe the horror of a people separated from God.

The rare Hebrew word for *darkness* used here appears in only three other places. In Psalm 82:5, the psalmist speaks of the judgment of the "gods": "The 'gods' know nothing, they understand nothing. They walk about in darkness; all the foundations of the earth are shaken." They stumble about in the blackness, judges who cannot see the way. This is the darkness of a terrifying loss of bearings and moral underpinnings.

Later, the word appears in Isaiah 8:22: False advisors will look "toward the earth and see only distress and darkness and fearful gloom, and they will be thrust into utter darkness." This darkness is a profound, terrifying, inexpressible void. Beautifully, this passage of darkness precedes the astounding proclamation in Isaiah 9, "There will be no more gloom for those who were in distress. . . . The people walking in darkness have seen a great light; on those living in the land of deep darkness a light has dawned" (Isa. 9:1–2).

No more gloom! Darkness meets its match! In fact, mercy and miracle welcome us in the only other biblical usage of the word translated *darkness*. The psalmist says of God, in Psalm 139:12, "For darkness is as light to you." In this brilliant contrast between thick and dreadful darkness and God, we find the aid and hope we seek. The dark vortex of sin, of moral blindness and unhinged morality, the sense of being suffocated by the dark, cannot compare with the light that is our God. Darkness, all that is wrong with the world, all the gasping hopelessness, cannot quench God's light. In fact, in God's presence, all darkness is vanquished and light, only light, remains.

God did not leave Abram in the thick and dreadful darkness. The Lord came to him, prophesied the future enslavement in Egypt, and then promised the return of Abram's descendants to the land of promise.

And into that nighttime, a smoking firepot and a blazing torch appeared and passed between the sacrificial parts. God literally "cut" a covenant. Even as Abram cut the sacrifices, so God cut a covenant, a deal, with Abram. Only this kind of covenant guaranteed both sides, which we see fulfilled in Jesus. "In him was life, and that life was the light of all" (John 1:4).

Thick and dreadful darkness? It can't smother the Light of the World who came, centuries later. "The light shines in the darkness, and the darkness has not overcome it" (John 1:5). The light of all.

TRAVELING MERCY

Dear one,
It is dark,
Sometimes thick and dreadfully dark.
But darkness
And light
Are the same to me.
And I can see in the dark
And past the dark.
Look to the east—
Light has dawned,
The shadows flee,
My Son is here,
The Light of the World.
And you need never
Walk in darkness
Or fall into thick and dreadful
Darkness
Ever again.

NOTE TO SELF

Thick and dreadful darkness
can't extinguish God's light.
No matter what.

APRIL 9

A GREAT LIGHT

> The people walking in darkness have seen a great light;
> on those living in the land of deep darkness a light has dawned.
>
> —Isaiah 9:2

Don't we all have those days of thick and dreadful darkness? Or nights? Or weeks? The dark panic when the phone rings and you lunge from bed and land on the floor, your heart thudding out of your chest. The nights when you sleep in your clothes waiting for the call. The test result with the implications you never expected. The pain of an injured child or shattered relationship. The knock at the door and the papers you never thought would be served.

Thick and dreadful darkness.

In the daytime, we can shoo away the birds of prey that flap their huge wings over our sacrifices, the sacrifices of time, money, love, and work. We hear their wings beat through the air and we prepare for their talons. But underneath our love offerings, sometimes, honestly, there's a bit of resentment. We work so hard, and still the vultures? The carrion eaters come clawing?

But in the night, when our defenses sleep, we are at the mercy of the darkness, the deep and dreadful dark that plagues us with nightmares and regret, fear and discouragement.

For Abram, surely the darkness was complicated by exhaustion. He chased around the covenantal land in battle, trying to save his kidnapped kin. He faced challenges as never before, left all his familiar surroundings, and followed this unknown and certainly unusual God. He waited for fruit on a promised family tree and so far couldn't glimpse the slightest hope of a branch.

Exhaustion compounds our thick, dreadful darkness. Exhaustion, whether physical or emotional or spiritual, lowers our resistance to discouragement, depression, and all manner of ills. Exhaustion from too many battles. Too much conflict. Or too few good calories (or too many bad ones). Exhaustion from loneliness, from pain.

But exhaustion alone doesn't equal thick and dreadful. The dreadful thickness of this dark is also about abandonment, the possibility or even the near reality of annihilation. Thick and dreadful, as in judged and found wanting not just by another human being, but even, perhaps, by God. Separated from others at the heart, because of your heart. It is a lostness incomparable and indescribable.

But it is a lostness that begs finding.

And our God finds us, comes looking for us. Our God who in the very beginning separated the darkness from the light and then turned on the light for us all by sending Jesus, the Light of the World. And then, as if that alone weren't the most amazing deliverance from the thick and dreadful darkness, from the gloom of walking in midnight during the middle of the day, Jesus turned the light on us and says, "You are the light of the world." Don't set your light under the table or under a barrel. Set it on a hill for everyone to see.

Like a lighthouse. Like stars in the sky.

Because the people who sat in darkness have seen a great light. And then become light in the darkness. And the darkness cannot overcome the light.

TRAVELING MERCY
Dear one,
Of course you are tired.
The way is long and steep,
And the night dark and deep.
But rest in my care,
For I have overcome the world
And hold it in my hands.
I sort out the dark
From the light,
And then the light rules both
Day and night.
Do you see it?
Even now
The light is dawning,
The sunrise from on high.

NOTE TO SELF
God's light rules. God's light wins.

APRIL 10

THE BACK-UP PLAN

> Now Sarai, Abram's wife, had borne him no children.
> But she had an Egyptian slave named Hagar.
>
> —Genesis 16:1

Not long after God reconfirmed the covenant with Abram, Sarai stated, "The Lord has kept me from having children" (v. 2). So she hatched herself a plan, arranging for Abram to sleep with her servant Hagar, who was probably a gift from the misguided trip to Egypt. This might have been culturally and legally acceptable at the time, with any child of the union belonging to the original couple. It would also eradicate the seeming infertility curse.

But the God who promised the couple a child never reneged on the promise. Sarai just wasn't looking at the real God. She looked at the gods of her past, not at the God of her present and her future. Isn't this the source of so many of our mistakes? We are looking, not at the one true God, but at one of the gods of our own past, of our culture, of the false belief systems surrounding us. And then the ripple effect of misguided intentions rolls out into a tidal wave, disrupting others' lives.

How might it have been if Sarai had focused on the true God and the promises made throughout the sojourn? What if she'd left well enough alone and waited a little while longer (say, thirteen years or so) for God to deliver on the promise of a child?

Or, having harangued Abram long enough, and badgered him into fulfilling the promise on her terms, what if Sarai decided to live with the mess she'd made rather than abuse the victim of the mess, Hagar, and later on, Hagar's son (see Gen. 16:1–6)? To punish Hagar so much that she ran away defeated Sarai's purpose in the first place: to provide an heir and a nation from her husband's loins.

But that's the way of it. When our plan works better than we expected (read: we get worse than we expected and are sorry we set it up ourselves), it's so tempting to blame someone else for the way it works. Sarai blamed Abram, and she blamed Hagar. It'd be easy to imagine her as a harsh woman, given what we've seen of her (and Abram's treatment of her) thus far. But sometimes when you know someone's back story, their behavior makes complete sense.

What if Sarai hadn't connived? An entire nation wouldn't have been born through Ishmael. What if Sarai hadn't run off Hagar, and instead had accepted Hagar as Abram's other wife and Ishmael as her own son? Maybe there wouldn't have been the long-term prophecy, "He will be a wild donkey of a man; his hand will be against everyone and everyone's hand against him, and he will live in hostility toward all his brothers" (Gen. 16:12).

Maybe a whole lot of unholy "holy wars" wouldn't have been fought between the two nations that descended from these half-brothers. Maybe a lot of bloodshed and grief and separation and pain and judgment would have been avoided.

Maybe. Maybe not.

We have no idea the long-term consequences of our behavior. But we do know that the influence of respect or disrespect pumps into other people's lives. Our actions help or hinder. We bless or we blunder.

Before we try to fulfill God's promises with our own plans and hands, maybe we could stop and wait a minute. Or a week. Or a year. Or thirteen. Because, as the psalmist would write years later, "The LORD is trustworthy in all he promises and faithful in all he does" (Ps. 145:13).

We under-believe in the mighty possibilities and promises God offers. We undersell God. Maybe we can learn to wait from the triangle of Abram-Sarai-Hagar. Wait for God, whose plans are far better than anything we mortals could imagine.

TRAVELING MERCY
Dear one,
I have such good plans,
And my timing will work out
Perfectly.
But it's hard to trust
On your timetable
Isn't it?
I do understand
That it's hard to wait,
But wait anyway.
You won't be sorry if you wait.
You might be sorry
If you don't.
Don't undersell my promises.
You can't over-believe in me.
If you can hand over your dreams to me,

I promise to handle them gently
And to hand them back
In just the right time.

NOTE TO SELF
Dream. Trust. Walk. Repeat.

APRIL 11

A WANDERER

> The angel of the LORD found Hagar near a spring in the desert.
> —GENESIS 16:7

Maybe you landed in the desert through no clear fault of your own. Someone else's defection, or desperation, acted on you. Now you wonder how you're going to survive. You seethe with anger that you bear on your own body or soul, or both, wounds from someone else. Those blisters on your feet formed because of another's unfaithfulness. You can fill in the blanks of the story, your story, because we all claim parts of this story as our own.

We are not alone. This is Hagar's story, as well. Hagar, of Abram and Sarai fame. Hagar became the human answer to a couple who couldn't stand trusting God any longer. Hagar found herself in her master's arms and his bed. Hagar couldn't refuse. And then the destruction of sin flooded upon her. She despised her mistress, and the feeling was returned full throttle in Sarai's bitterness and jealousy. Sarai mistreated Hagar, who fled into the wilderness. Unless something happened, she would die there.

The sense of annihilation in the desert, of being invisible, unnecessary, and forgotten, looms over our emotional horizon.

Haven't we all been there, part of the abandoned ones? Maybe an entire litany of instances fills your lungs. But before we blow our pity party horns, maybe we can recognize the inevitability of abandonment. Of course people will hurt us, and in our exile, whether self-imposed or other imposed, we wind up alone and terrified. And maybe a tiny bit angry.

Maybe Hagar had some time to think while hanging out there in the desert. She was both victim and victimizer. She despised Sarai; Sarai abused her; Hagar ran away. We land in desert straits often because we're a link in the chain reaction of sin. But perhaps the sin and lack of faith in the story began before Hagar entered the picture. Hagar was an Egyptian. During that famine, Abram trudged off to Egypt. But maybe God wasn't telling Abram to go to Egypt; maybe Abram's terror of starvation and his responsibility for his wife and entourage sent him packing and tracking that direction (terror seems, on the surface, quite reasonable). And Egypt didn't go all that well for Sarai—her fear-filled husband handed her over to Pharaoh to be his wife. Another link in the chain. So Sarai ended up with this souvenir from Egypt called Hagar, and every time she saw her servant, she remembered.

It helps to understand the road traveled and the people who acted upon us in our story. It helps to understand some of the reasons for their actions. It helps to realize that none of us are blameless en route on this movement toward freedom. But to be locked in blame is to be self-imprisoned, and blame is one prison to which we alone hold the key.

Sometimes, resources wait within reach. When the angel found Hagar, she'd camped out near a spring. Maybe, while we wait in the desert, certain this isn't freedom's route, God could open our eyes to the spring nearby. Life-sustaining water to tide us over. Maybe that spring will spring the lock on our desert experience, spring us from our self-imposed prison of blame. But even so, we can't stay there forever. That angel found Hagar and ordered her to go back.

Maybe there are angels in our places of abandonment as well. A cloud of the unseen, tending to our needs and moving us forward. Or back, as with Hagar. Her name, it turns out, means "wanderer, emigrant." The angel was telling her to resist that unfortunate moniker and to return to Abram and Sarai. Not to blame, but rather, changed. A wanderer no longer.

TRAVELING MERCY
To my wandering one,
There is a spring nearby, if you will but drink
Even as you think through
The chain of events
Leading to this abandoned place,
This exile of sorts.
You are but one link,
But a significant one.
And rather than blame
Those you've despised
And those you've encountered,
Instead consider your own role,
And let me change you,
Spring you
From the prison of blame.

NOTE TO SELF
I can blame others or watch for water.

APRIL 12

ONE WHO SERVES

"Go back to your mistress and submit to her."
—Genesis 16:9

Sarai's big plan worked: She sent Abram to bed the maid, and surprise! The maid conceived. Hagar woke up sick as a dog, pregnant, and miserable. And Sarai realized her own folly. Why had she given Hagar the privilege of bearing a child for Abram, the man who'd dragged Sarai all over the continent with the promise of a child of her own? She'd conceived a plan, but the plan backfired because it didn't really satisfy her own longings: to bear the child promised her.

So she bullied Hagar enough to make Hagar doubly miserable.

Of all the news Hagar expected to receive in her desert dash, the angel's words weren't the preferred message. "Go back to your mistress and submit to her"? Not quite. No way. The last thing she wanted was to crawl back to her jealous mistress and submit to her. The last thing most of us want is to submit to anyone.

Another's insolence doesn't justify mistreatment from us. And regardless of the many definitions for the word *mistreatment* in the Hebrew language (from a mocking laugh all the way to physical abuse), this passage is not a blanket statement about returning to an abuser. This is not a missive from God to order all people to put themselves in a position of battery.

In Hagar's specific situation, God said to return. But in a general sense, all questions of abuse aside, submission to a person in authority requires strength of character. To submit means, essentially, to put ourselves lower than the other person. To allow them to not only be in charge over us, but to be valued over us.

And then our complex self-esteem issues rise up and assert themselves. "They have no right," we say. "They aren't worthy." "How dare they think they are so important?" we ask. "I don't deserve this treatment." "They are not the boss of me." And on it goes. Submission is not a statement of our worth. It is not a statement of the other's worth. It is simply a heart attitude that views another as more important than ourselves. Our self-esteem needn't get involved at all.

Submission is actually a statement about our worth in God's sight. Because God loves us, we can, with joy, submit to others in authority over us.

Look at what we know of Christ, with our longer view of Scripture: He lowered himself to become a human being. He took the guise of a servant, and even told the disciples, "I am among you as one who serves" (Luke 22:27).

Hagar returned to serve Sarai in an act of supreme courage and confidence: not in her mistress, not in herself. Confidence in the God who sees, the God who preserves. The God who calls us and provides water in the deserts of our lives. The God who would one day walk among us, serving us.

TRAVELING MERCY

Dear one,
If you enter every relationship
Secure in my love for you
And my care for you,
Another's treatment of you
Will matter very little.
Because what I say about you
Is the truth.
So don't be afraid
To honor another.
Don't feel you need to defend
Your own honor.
Just serve with all your heart,
With all my heart,
And keep carving the blessing trail
For others to
Follow.

NOTE TO SELF

Lord, help me serve from the overflow of your love.

APRIL 13

THE GOD WHO HEARS

"You are now pregnant and you will give birth to a son.
You shall name him Ishmael, for the Lord has heard of your misery."

—Genesis 16:11

When Hagar hauled off to the desert of Shur, she wasn't shooting out like a surprise bullet from an unaimed gun. She was no child running away from home, always looking behind her for her parents to rescue her and change their wicked ways. No, the caravan route through Shur led straight to Egypt. Hagar, the wanderer, the emigrant, was headed back home. She ran from her present pain, to return to her past.

Shur means wall, or enclosure, perhaps so-called because of the mountain ranges that rise up like a wall alongside the caravan route to Egypt. There, the mountains enclosed her, offering a bit of protection, and served as a compass for the route back to Egypt. Alone, abandoned, terrified, and angry, with every step she must have thought, "I'm a little closer to home. I can make it. Just one more day." Maybe she even kept a watch for people she knew heading from Egypt.

All she heard were her own fears and anger. The tapes played repeatedly in her memory: of her treatment at the hands of Sarai and her abandonment by Abram. But returning home was not to be. For the first time in recorded history, an angel appeared in the narrative, halting the servant's flight back to Egypt. Graciously, God broke into the reruns in her soul and spoke to her in this most desperate of deserts, with her body bearing the seed of someone else's lack of faith. The angel found Hagar near a spring in the desert. The angel asked, "Where have you come from, and where are you going?" (Gen. 16:8).

This two-fold question helps us get our bearings, helps us figure out a flight plan. Only if we know where we've come from can we begin to figure out where we're headed. But Hagar answered only the first question: "I'm running away from my mistress Sarai."

It was answer enough for the angel, who ordered her to return. Not to Egypt, but to the friction-riddled tents of Abram and Sarai. "Go back to your mistress and submit to her."

Hagar was desperate for deliverance—but not this kind of deliverance. Sarai might have been the last person Hagar wanted to encounter, let alone submit to.

But the angel didn't just ship her back into trouble. Instead, God spoke into her imprisoning despair, promising her a future with descendants too numerous to count. Then the angel named the son Hagar carried in her womb, "Ishmael," meaning, "God hears."

"I hear," God said. In the midst of her sense of annihilation, having lost everything, Hagar heard from this God of the desert, this God who hears. She called God, "You are the God who sees me," and said in wonder, "I have now seen the One who sees me." Every time she felt the baby kick and prod in her womb, she remembered "God hears." Every time Sarai mistreated her, she could remind herself, "God sees." In her lonely nights and long days, she could whisper, "God hears. God sees."

Cast out of Abram's arms and his home and into the arms of the God who hears. The One who sees.

Hagar, part victim in the story, emerged from the desert with a double blessing. Seeing the God who sees her and knowing that same God would provide for her and her child.

Despair can morph into despising for us too and destroy the possible blessing. In the desert of Shur, Hagar had a choice, and so do we. The challenge is to not sin in the desert, though we feel betrayed and cast off and abandoned. Deserted in the desert. And that very sense of despair and desertion can close our eyes and ears to the presence of God.

It is a lie, because the God of the desert sees and hears us.

May you see the God who sees you, looks at you, and loves you. "I see you," God says. "I hear you." If we choose, the desert will give us eyes to see, ears to hear.

TRAVELING MERCY
Dear one,
I see you there by the road,
Stranded
In the desert of Shur.
Your own desert is anything but sure.
But I am sure
That I see you.
And I want you to see me
Seeing you.
I am the God who hears.

So tell me.
And let me open your eyes
So you can see me
And your ears
So you can hear me
As clearly as you can hear
The water in the spring
By the road to Shur.
I see you.
I hear you.
I love you.
Do you
See me
Seeing you?

NOTE TO SELF
God finds me, sees me, hears me, leads me.

APRIL 14

THE YEARS IN REVIEW

> When Abram was ninety-nine years old,
> the LORD appeared to him.
>
> —GENESIS 17:1

Another thirteen years crawled past, years of Abram shaking his head and wondering what on earth was happening (or more like, what wasn't happening) and had he been foolish to believe in this promise? His wife wasn't pregnant, wasn't likely to ever be, not at this age. Now for a whopping quarter of a century, Abram had been holding on to this impossible and ridiculous promise. Maybe he'd gotten to the place of never talking about the dream, about the calling, because he was so far from what he'd expected. On his own timeline, he should be bouncing grandbabies on his knee by now.

Why had he given up everything to follow that strange unknown voice from pillar to post and back again? Why was he still peering out over the horizon in expectancy, believing that the promise might yet come to fruition? Did he really think that his wife, barren for nearly a century, and now decades past the "way of women," would have a child?

Of all the improbable promises. Easier to believe that Ishmael was the fulfillment of the promise all along. Easier to just raise him, hope for the best, and keep the uneasy truce between the wives, Hagar with her young, firm flesh, and Sarai with her wrinkles and drooping skin.

Isn't it true for us, as well? What promise have you held on to for years? Do we really know what it is to hope and hope and never experience the fulfillment? How do we continue to hold on when God so seldom appears, when the nights are long and the vultures swoop in on our dreams?

And isn't it easy to just stop trying to rev up belief in a promise? After all, the world gave up on you long ago. Aren't you tired of being the drum major, whipping up a parade when the world wants to just disband the band? Common sense told Abram, and tells us, that there is nothing to the promise anymore, that hope melts like snow in the desert and disappears, our optimism sinking through the sandy-bottom floor of our soul.

But since when does common sense get to define a miracle? Since never. So, how did Abram hold on to the promise, the impossibility of a miracle?

Maybe he revisited the altars he had built after encounters with God, those places where God reaffirmed the promise and reconfirmed his presence in the world. We can do that. Maybe he remembered the victories, like the routing of the kings and getting Lot back from captivity. Maybe Abram reviewed the specifics of his relationship with this God, who called out of the blue and never let him forget it. Maybe every time this man's soul wilted in the desert heat of discouragement and delay, he spoke the truth out loud, calling it out over the grounds before him, shouting it to the horizon.

Maybe we can do the same.

Remember the promise.

Revisit the altars.

Reconfirm God's presence.

Remember the victories.

Review the relationship with God.

And then speak it out over your world. Shout it, if need be. But grab the hem of God's garment, the promise of God's presence, and never let go. Because the promise comes from the One who said, "I am God Almighty." Abraham's promise, our promise. Don't ever forget: God promised.

TRAVELING MERCY

Dear one,
I haven't forgotten you.
I cannot forget you,
And I shall never forget you.
So remember this
All the times you doubt—
Remember when you've seen my hand,
Remember when you've known my presence,
Remember when we've won battles together,
Review what you know to be true.
Because it's true
I will never forget you.

NOTE TO SELF

When I doubt the future,
I'll remember God's presence in the past.

APRIL 15

I WILL CHANGE YOUR NAME

> "No longer will you be called Abram; your name will
> be Abraham, for I have made you a father of many nations."
>
> —Genesis 17:5

Names, thoughtfully given, are meant to describe us or give us a characteristic to grow into. I loved one name in particular for one of our children, but discarded it when I realized it meant "bent nose." Why give a child a name like that? What was there to live up to, after all? "Become a prize fighter and get your nose busted, honey, and you'll have succeeded." Or, "Just be really uncoordinated and fall often enough, and you'll live up to your name."

We carry so many names for ourselves that weren't part of our birth moniker. Like regret. Or failure. Incompetent, thoughtless, slow, dull, fragile, problem child, troublemaker, black sheep. We have our own pet names for ourselves, except a pet you'd never want to adopt or, well, pet. But names stick, whether we label ourselves or others do, whether the names gained traction in the birthing room, on the playground, at home, at school, or at work. And under those names we labor, carrying residual shame, secretly disliking ourselves or parts of ourselves. Or not so secretly, because we are quick to let others in on our incapacities.

Remember those sticky labels, meant to introduce ourselves at meetings and conventions and parties? "Hello, my name is . . ." they boast in big bright print. Fill in the blank with how you feel about yourself, how you see yourself, or how other people have labeled you throughout your years. Hello, my name is Shame. Hello, my name is Disappointment. Hello, my name is Underachiever. Hello my name is Sad or Disappointed or Rejected or Loser or Failure.

Wait with that nametag for a minute.

And then see what God did for Abram. Just when he was about to give up on God, God showed up in Abram's life again. It had been a long wait, longer still by the silent heavens, with no recorded interaction with God during that time. Thirteen years of waiting, and of watching Ishmael grow up after they connived that birth. Thirteen years, knowing with every passing month the likelihood of God paying off the promissory shrank. Thirteen years of Abram wondering if he'd misunderstood, if Ishmael was the promised child after all. Thirteen long years.

For ninety-nine years, Abram dragged around the name that meant "exalted father." His name pointed backward to his own father and lineage, not to his own status. But no doubt he wearied of the raised eyebrows when he and his aged wife walked past or when they crawled out of their tent creaking and groaning. The son of the exalted father, a man with a barren wife, a princess who sometimes behaved decidedly un-princess like.

But one day, the Lord reappeared to Abram. After reintroductions ("I am God Almighty") and reinstructions ("walk before me and be blameless"), God reconfirmed the covenant.

Though Abram didn't have that promised child yet, he still got a new name as a reality check. From now on, people would call him Abraham, "Father of many nations." Perhaps they would have a new look in their eyes, one of expectancy. And Abraham could look in the mirror and remind himself of the truth: "I am the father of many nations." More than that, he could remind himself of the One who bestowed such an outlandish promise. God Almighty, the creator of heaven and earth, promised. A new name as proof of the promise.

So what is your new name, your proof of the promise? What if you rewrite your name badge? So it says, "Hello, my name is _____." And fill in the blank with God's word for you.

TRAVELING MERCY
Dear one,
What will it be,
Your new name?
Rip off the old label,
Look to the heavens,
Count the stars,
See how great my love
Is for you.
And then consider
What will you be called?
How about
"Mine"?

NOTE TO SELF
I belong to God. Others' labels are irrelevant.

APRIL 16

LIVING INTO THE NAME

A good name is more desirable than great riches.
—Proverbs 22:1

Babies get their own name at birth. Children are often renamed at adoption. Both constitute significant life changes for the children. And naming, as we read in Genesis 2:19–20, is a sign of authority over the animal or person being named. So when God changed Abram's name to Abraham, God exercised authority over this man who would become the father of many nations. But God also signified that Abraham's life would take a new direction.

Abram's change of name couldn't have come at a more perfect time. His joints ached, but not more than his heart. He creaked and cracked as he played ball with Ishmael, and was exhausted by the inevitable tussles of a growing and energetic boy, to say nothing of the palpable tension in his home. No doubt he wondered why God waited so long to deliver the promised child. It sure would have been easier to play tag if he were a younger man. A lot younger. But that's part of the joy of a new name, given by God: God fuels the miracle of living into the name.

A change of direction. And for Sarai, too (see Gen. 17:15). Her life changed entirely when God changed her name. Her new name, like Abraham's, broke with her past, pointing her toward a new future. The change from Sarai to Sarah marked a significant turning point in her life. Not just a mother! A mother of nations! Kings of countries would descend from her.

But naming also revokes the power of the old name, the identity associated with it. Abraham's name became a prophecy and promise, not a recap of his past.

Naming equals claiming. We name our puppy, the puppy comes to us, running, tumbling, and drooling, ears flapping. Our puppy. We name our babies, they turn their heads when we call them, and hopefully come running, tumbling, and drooling (but without their ears flapping). When Abraham declared his name to be Ishmael, he claimed him as his son.

When we name someone or something, we exercise authority over it. To name our own labels of ourselves, or of someone else, removes some of the power of those labels. Bringing hidden words into the foreground diminishes their strength, like a hurricane petering out when it runs out of water. For instance, we stop feeding the hurricane of shame with the dirty water of silent acceptance and submission to the shame label.

To name a child in the ancient Near East meant to direct the child's destiny. Notice the tense of God's promise to Abraham. God didn't say, "I *will* make you a father of many nations." God said, "I *have* made you a father of many nations." Whether we live in the present reality of a promise fulfilled or not, God's promise stands outside of our current situation. In God's timing, the promise to Abraham was already true.

The promises made to us are already true as well. We begin to live into the names God gives us. Like, Child of God. Chosen by God. Remembered by God. Delighted in by God. Sung over by God.

Names help us live up. And live into. And live it up.

TRAVELING MERCY
Dear one,
Take my new name
For you:
Chosen one,
Child in whom I delight,
Child of the Promise,
Peculiar treasure,
Priest and king,
Beloved.
I know your name
And I know your heart
And I love you.
In fact
I have inscribed you
On the palm of my hand.
I will never forget.

NOTE TO SELF
Live into God's name for me: Child of God.

APRIL 17

SIGN OF THE COVENANT

"This is my covenant with you and your descendants after you,
the covenant you are to keep. . . . You are to undergo circumcision,
and it will be the sign of the covenant between me and you."

—Genesis 17:10–11

God made extensive promises to Abraham throughout their journey together. When it came time to ratify the covenant, God reiterated those promises (see Gen. 17:1–8) and then had just one requirement for Abraham. God said, "Here is your side of the covenant, Abraham. You'll be circumcised, you and every other male in your family and household."

Abraham leaped up to fulfill his side of the promise, which is astounding when you think about it. But the sign of Abraham's covenant with God was far more than the flesh wound he sustained. Throughout history, Abraham was revered as a man of obedience, a man who obeyed God without hesitation. Circumcision became the outward sign of a people who followed and obeyed God, a people whose hearts were fixed on God.

How do we even know this, and how do people whose hearts are fixed on God act? Centuries later, Moses, the great leader of the Israelites, said, "Circumcise your hearts, therefore, and do not be stiff-necked any longer" (see Deut. 10:14–20).

Why did Moses say *therefore*? Because though everything belongs to God, our heavenly God set his affection on the Israelites and loved them and chose them. And this God, "the great God, mighty and awesome . . . shows no partiality and accepts no bribes," this God, "defends the cause of the fatherless and the widow, and loves the foreigner residing among you, giving them food and clothing. And you are to love those who are foreigners . . ." (Deut. 10:17–19).

Say that again? Circumcision of the heart looks like what?

Like loving our neighbor, even if our neighbor is an alien, foreign to us, different from us. No wonder Jesus showed up and said the two most important rules are to love God and love people. Small wonder that Jesus could say, "If you were Abraham's children, then you would do what Abraham did" (John 8:39).

No wonder Abraham became renowned as a man of hospitality and kindness. No wonder he jumped up after circumcision and served the three guests, one of whom turned out to be the Lord. No wonder he welcomed Lot into his household to live, in spite of Lot's undeserving status. No wonder he fought the kings for Lot and gave Lot the best land. No wonder he interceded for Lot.

Because Abraham, the first man of the covenant of circumcision, bore in his heart the encircling of God's love for him. And that translated into a life of service. A life of living out love. A life of obedience coming from being loved.

No wonder Paul said in Galatians 5:6, "For in Christ Jesus neither circumcision nor uncircumcision has any value. The only thing that counts is faith expressing itself through love."

The only thing that counts.

TRAVELING MERCY
Dear one,
I'm so very excited
To consider what this world will look like
As more and more
You love as I love
And more and more
You care for those who are excluded,
The have-nots,
Can-nots,
Do-nots.
Faith
That I love you
Expressing itself
Through the way you love.
It's a perfect circle,
This circumcision of your heart.

NOTE TO SELF
Today, watch for and bless the foreigner.
Even if it's me.

APRIL 18

ONLY THE BEST WILL DO

> He said, "If I have found favor in your eyes,
> my lord, do not pass your servant by."
>
> —Genesis 18:3

Pretend you've just been circumcised (sorry, imagining that is beyond me, unless it's like giving birth). Three strangers show up at your favorite tree. Wouldn't you wave weakly and gesture them over toward where you sit in pain? Or even close your eyes and hope they keep walking past?

But Abraham bounded to his feet and ran over to the strangers. Not hobbled, crawled, limped, or moaned and groaned. He immediately welcomed them as guests. It was inconvenient and terrible timing, undoubtedly, for drop-ins. But this man's huge heart opened further and he offered his best provisions to these visitors.

Whether we are recovering from surgery, from a miserable day at a job we dislike, from a fight with a family member, or from a day in the life, few are the times when we leap to our feet and rush to the door to invite strangers for lunch. And if we had to bake the bread while they waited, and run behind the house to slaughter the main entrée, how likely are we to say, "Come on in"?

Plus, what about the risk involved? What might the strangers do to our family? Or our knickknacks, family heirlooms, and the safe that isn't bolted to the floor?

In spite of hospitality standards in those days, with many miles between towns, food, lodging, and news, Abraham had a good deal to lose by inviting these people into his life. But, it turns out, they were there on heavenly business, with a parcel better than a Publisher's Clearing House check. Promise fulfillment, we could call it.

Abraham, renowned in Jewish tradition for his hospitality and kindness, bowed low. He, a wealthy nomad, blessed beyond all reason with goods and a trophy wife and more animals lowing in the fields than he could count, bowed low, as a servant to a master, a slave to his owner. He didn't consider himself to be doing the travelers a favor. They would favor him, in fact, if they would stop for a visit.

Stop, that is, and let Abraham serve them. "Lord, do not pass your servant by" (Gen. 18:3).

All this, just after circumcision, his own and all the men and boys in his household and fields. There wasn't a male person free from pain. But they rallied and brought water to let the guests wash up. Sarah, who stood behind the tent flaps, hurried to whip up some bread and set it to a fast rise and bake. A servant dashed behind the tent for a fresh catch, slaughtering the animal and roasting it.

This is no small offer of hospitality. It's not a cup of water while they wait on the porch. It's a half-day of preparation, involving many people in the process. And in turn, involving them all in the gift.

With the meal served, Abraham stood behind the guests while they ate, like a butler straight out of an English manor house, eager to tend any needs that arose, not counting on any personal gain for himself. And here's something else: Abraham did not even know whom he served that day.

A lesson from Abraham's life. Happy to serve, no matter who strolls past. May we say with Abraham, "Please do not pass your servant by." And then live into the blessing, and live out the blessing.

TRAVELING MERCY
Dear one,
And what would you say
If you didn't know who knocked on your door?
"Do not pass your servant by"?
What if you didn't know it was angels sent from heaven?
What if you didn't know
If they'd rob you blind, these strangers?
What if you didn't know?
Would you still say,
"Let a little water be brought for your feet"?
"Bake the bread, slaughter the calf"?
Would you still provide your very best
Even if you didn't know?
Because you never know
When you are entertaining angels
Unawares.

NOTE TO SELF
Live in and live out God's welcome.

APRIL 19

NEIGHBORING

"Let me get you something to eat, so you can be refreshed and then go on your way—now that you have come to your servant."

—Genesis 18:5

"People just don't neighbor anymore," a friend said when I visited her farm. We lounged on the deck, the wide expanse of fields, hills, and sky spread out before us. "Every neighbor is a square mile from the next, and we don't see each other like we used to." Living on a farm is like living in the wilderness was for Abraham, perhaps. Drop-in guests are rare these days, whether in city, village, or countryside.

This woman decided to do something to change that. A major ice cream brand was offering a free ice cream sundae party to the person who composed the most convincing essay about ice cream and community and why he or she deserved a great big sundae-fest. My friend wrote about her neighbors, and the importance of neighboring, and how she wanted to invite everyone within a multiple-mile radius to a big shindig on her farm. She would provide a huge buffet of food, if the company would donate the ice cream.

She won the essay contest. Nearly a hundred neighbors showed up. Cars, trucks, tractors, bikes, even a tricycle or two packed the yard. Spanning many generations, and representing thousands of years of living, guests arrived on foot, in strollers, with walkers and canes, and my friend, who is seventy-five, greeted every single one of them at the edge of the drive. She provided a spread of food covering two tables, which groaned with barbeque and side dishes, and loaded with her homemade desserts to accompany the copious quantities of ice cream and toppings. A fiddler played and a caller directed a square dance and a circle dance. It was a day to remember—to remember neighborliness, kindness, joy, and feasting. That day, people neighbored, and they feasted on the joy of companionship in a world compromised by isolation.

She did not expect payback, and neither, I think, did Abraham. He rushed to greet his drop-in guests and then hurried about preparing the finest food for them. He ran around like a servant and provided enormous quantities of the best food he could offer, then stood off to the side, smiling, enjoying his guests enjoying themselves.

Perhaps the payback is the joy of serving, the joy of satisfying multiple needs simultaneously: the need of community, the need for food, and the need for acceptance and love. The scent of roasted barbeque and oozing fruit cobblers. Laughter ringing off the barn rafters and finding a home in lonely hearts. And a little fiddle throwing out some foot-tapping music.

It's party time. Got any neighbors?

TRAVELING MERCY

Dear one,
Do you hear the sound of laughter,
The party,
The music,
The boot-scooting,
The roundup?
Do you smell the roasting meat
And the bubbling cobblers
And the sweet incense of people together?
Do you feel the rumble
Along the floorboards
That says
"God is near"?
Because I am
Every time you say
"Welcome neighbor"
And throw a little party
In my name.

NOTE TO SELF
Even a smile extends God's welcome.

APRIL 20

THIS TIME NEXT YEAR

> Then one of them said, "I will surely return to you about this time next year, and Sarah your wife will have a son."
>
> —Genesis 18:10

Probably if I were eighty-nine, after a lifetime of barrenness and just as long spent warding off bitterness, and after an awful lot of monthly checks to see if I were, in fact, going to be part of the big promise God made, I'd have eavesdropped on the guests from behind the tent flap too. And I'd have laughed in a strange combination of elation and absurdity. "Is this really to be? Did he mean us, Abraham?" After all these years, would Sarah and Abraham really cradle a baby in their long-empty, longing arms?

Yes, the visitors said. After all these years, the impossible would become possible, the implausible and statistically ridiculous would become reality.

So rarely do we hear a specific word from God, such a promise pinpointed, like, "This time next year you will be rocking your own baby." How often do we get a detailed timeline, or even a personalized promise for that matter? "You will have an entire nation come from you." "Kings and queens will be born from your line." In fact, it might be hard to even figure out what our promise is, and how will we know that it is fulfilled, if we haven't isolated the promise?

Perhaps a page from Sarah's book is that waiting will be rewarded, and God is not limited by age, not hindered by our lack of sight, not thwarted by our feeble faith. God doesn't change, and God is the one who said, in light of Abraham and Sarah's incredulity, "Is anything too hard for the LORD?" (Gen. 18:14).

No, no, no. A thousand times no. We see from these early chronicles that nothing, absolutely nothing, is too hard for the Lord. We read, throughout the Scriptures, of impossible feats and daring acts that strain our belief system and challenge our faith. God consistently upholds the standard of doing the impossible.

So today, turn toward your impossible list. What's on it? And who? Or do you even have a list? If not, start your impossible list. God delights to do the impossible, and nothing is far-fetched for God when we look within the realms of God's will.

Maybe we could start with something close to home. Like a person with ADHD actually paying attention long enough to experience God's presence. (That'd be me, and that's a miracle when it happens.) Or, God turning a hard heart into one of malleable openness. Or, God healing a broken spirit.

What about that prayer list of impossibles? If barrenness is the lack of fruit, then fruitfulness is the opposite and the answer to that dilemma. Where does God want us to bear fruit? Fruit for his sake, fruit for the world's sake. Fruit that endures.

Faith will turn to sight. One day, all that we have prayed for and hoped for and held on for, all the people we offer up to the Lord, all the pain and the loss and the sorrow and tears—all of this waiting will make sense. Because nothing is too hard for the Lord.

Just ask Sarah.

TRAVELING MERCY
Dear one,
Say it again:
Nothing is impossible with the Lord.
Nothing is impossible with the Lord.
Nothing!
So try me and see.
Put your life,
Your fears,
Your dreams,
Your barrenness,
Your pain,
Your loved ones,
Your future,
And theirs,
Into my hands,
And watch me work the impossible.
It's how I roll.
Try me
And see.

NOTE TO SELF
Make an impossible list today.
Then walk into it.

APRIL 21

DANGER IN THE DESERT

> Sarah laughed to herself as she thought, "After I am
> worn out and my lord is old, will I now have this pleasure?"
>
> —Genesis 18:12

Worn out. Worn out from the journey. Worn out after following this God she couldn't see and this husband she could see. Worn out with hoping, month after month, that the promised child would be planted in her barren womb. Worn out from the wait, the walk, the wilderness. All that wear and tear is dangerous for our dreams. How tempting to force them, to connive to make our own dreams come true, in our own way. Like with Abraham and Sarah, who decided Hagar would be the answer to those dreams since Sarah seemingly wasn't able to fulfill them. Evidently, they thought, to their acute anguish, neither was God.

The other side of disappointment is to stop dreaming, to decide that we can't afford to dream, we can't risk more let down, we can't possibly cling to something so intangible. It's not wise, living in some fairy tale where dreams "really do come true." Calling a cease-fire on dreaming seems like common sense. Except that when we stop dreaming, we start dying. We stop really living, we stop looking forward, we stop scanning the horizon for possibilities and instead examine every pebble before us for problems. The people I know who have quit dreaming have quit growing. Suffocated, the tiny flame of hope dies.

I'm not sure that's good stewardship. But even so, the desert is a dangerous place for dreams. Perhaps, though, it may also be a refining place, where our dreams are brought into sharper focus, high-definition hopes. In the wide-open spaces, there is room for dreaming, for reimagining our future. Here, with endless horizons, our dreams too can embrace the possibilities.

Try listing your dreams thus far. You don't have to be super-spiritual and tell yourself that all you want is God, that God is enough for you. That is true, of course, for all of us at our deepest level.

Or maybe you haven't risked dreaming for a very long time, because the pain has been too great and others' dreams seem so much more important. Maybe you've been in relationships where there was only room for one dream, and it wasn't yours. Or dreaming is costly in your ledger because others' dreams have cost you dearly, perhaps financially as well as emotionally. And disappointment carries a steep cost. Sarah became angry and scheming in the face of a lifetime of monthly disappointments.

Did Abraham and Sarah worship the dream more than they worshiped God, the giver of the dream? Sometimes the dream becomes all we see, and we try to work everything to our advantage so that our dream can be fulfilled. After my first couple of books were released, publishers began to emphasize their authors' speaking platforms, their important connections, and how many books they were able to sell. This became my goal, and I looked at everyone as a possible source of its fulfillment. I lived on high alert constantly, looking for the next contact, the lead that would promote me into a different league. In my fear, I undercut some relationships and wounded people. My chest sometimes literally hurt with fear, because what if I missed the person or didn't find the perfect opportunity? I thought it all depended on me, and my heart palpitations were a dead giveaway.

And then came the desert. And the good news that it doesn't all depend on us. It all depends on God, on God's clear promise into that desert: "I will make nations of you, and kings will come from you" (see Gen. 17:6, 16). Now is a good time to name that pain of broken, unfulfilled dreams. We are free to dream here. We can invite God to bring our dreams to the surface again, to reseed our souls with his dreams.

We surrender our dreams and God gives us the world.

TRAVELING MERCY

Dear one,
Do you remember your dreams?
When you were small,
And dreaming was part of your work,
What did you dream
Of doing, of being, of becoming?
It's not too late.
It's never too late
To dream.
After all,
I am the God who raises the dead,

And that includes you
And your dreams.
If you are not dead
Then neither are your dreams.
Come back to life;
Come back to hope.
Come to me,
Your very great reward.
Find the freedom in the dream
And the dream of freedom.

NOTE TO SELF
Time to dream again.
The God who raises the dead can resurrect my dreams.

APRIL 22

SAVED IN SPITE OF OURSELVES

Then the LORD said, "Shall I hide from Abraham
what I'm about to do?"

—GENESIS 18:17

Picture at a ripe old age, say eighty-five, engaging in hand-to-hand combat with a bunch of other armies. All to take back a relative who has been less than loyal and less than righteous by all appearances. After all, the relative pitches his tent near Sin City, driving the tent pegs deep into the desert floor, and gets a crick in his neck ogling at all the happenings there (see Gen. 14). Years roll past, but the tomfoolery doesn't end with that classic case of lust. The man returns for another eyeful, buys a house, acquires a wife, and fathers unnamed and evidently expendable daughters.

Meanwhile, back at Abraham's tent, the three visitors swallow the last morsel of fresh-baked bread and tender meat. They tip their hats to Abraham, and then one who is eventually revealed to be the Lord says, "Should we let him in on our plan?"

Turns out, they're heading over to Vile Village to destroy it. Abraham goes on the alert, always concerned for his nephew. He enters into what my Jewish friends consider a classic case of bargaining with God, chipping away at the numbers until extracting the promise that God won't destroy the city if ten righteous people live there. Abraham throws himself into the gap, pleading for salvation, and convicts the rest of the world by his earnest pleas.

Judging by the smoke and sulfur that ensues, God comes up empty-handed in the search for righteousness. Even so, Lot's family leaves skid marks behind them as the angels literally drag them out of town. The sons-in-law refuse to leave, because they consider Lot a practical joker who never tells the truth about anything, let alone about fire and destruction or the importance of morality. Lot's unnamed wife turns for one last wistful gaze at the town as it starts to smolder, and for her unwillingness to leave the past behind turns into a salt deposit on the desert floor, the beginnings of the Dead Sea some say. And the nameless daughters? Downhill slope straight into despair and ultimately enmity from Abraham's extended family. It's a terrible family portrait.

We don't hear from Lot again in his lifetime, though the apostle Peter many years later assumes that because Lot was rescued he must have been righteous (see 2 Pet. 2:7). In spite of anything we see from his character, which doesn't lead us toward a beneficial definition of righteousness, God saved him.

And maybe that's the whole point of the story, right there. In spite of us, God saves us.

Because, really, no one is righteous. Not one. Except for Jesus, who would come centuries later to deliver us from our own fascination with Sin City.

TRAVELING MERCY
Dear one,
Less than loyal,
Less than righteous,
Less than perfect,
Less than loving,
Less than giving,
Less than forgiving.
Does that describe you,
Ever?
Perhaps.
But I forget
Because I have forgiven you,
And delivered you,
And am inviting you now
To leave your past alone.
Stop staring backward
And walk forward.
With me.

NOTE TO SELF
I can't walk forward if I'm always looking back.

APRIL 23

A PARENT'S MIDDLE-OF-THE-NIGHTMARE

> He looked down toward Sodom and Gomorrah, toward
> all the land of the plain, and he saw dense smoke rising
> from the land, like smoke from a furnace.
>
> —Genesis 19:28

Lot's story must rank high on the list of a parent's worst nightmares. You beg, you plead, you teach, you lead, you give, you intercede. And where does all this get you? Exactly nowhere. Your charge smiles a big smile and heads off to the horizon, the place that soon will be a smoking ruin. His version of the Promised Land is a downward plunge into decadence and disaster.

But more than a parent's worst nightmare. Worst heartbreak. Abraham did everything possible to raise this young man who'd been moved, lost his father, moved again and again, been kidnapped, and then terrorized by bullies. Granted, he'd acted like a spoiled child much of the time, taken the best land for himself, and moved to a place guaranteed to keep his addiction active and potentially deadly.

The one thing Abraham apparently didn't carry with him to compound his grief was regret. He had done everything except commit his nephew to rehab or lock him in a padded cell. He'd provided guidance and nurture, an arm around the shoulder, and business savvy. He'd demonstrated immense generosity and wisdom. And in the end, when Lot was lost to him, Abraham couldn't beat himself up for not having done enough.

A troublesome person can become the centerpiece of a family's life. With someone like Lot loitering in the halls of your house and littering the family room, while everyone else is earning their keep, the household begins to revolve around the latest "Lot" crisis. What Lot did or said, who he hurt or angered this time. What the principal said, or the police, or the doctor who'd prescribed painkillers to an addict. The latest tussle becomes the subject of the next conversation. Or every conversation.

It destroys families. It destroys marriages. It hurts the other kids in the household and damages other relationships.

People get trampled under the hooves of the crazymaker's crazy horse. It gets more and more difficult to decentralize family life from Lot.

Spinning Lot off onto his own land and into his own life was a stroke of genius, and the only sane move Abraham could have made. It's the hardest one possible, and Abraham later headed to the rescue after Lot's kidnapping. But that's the last recorded interaction between Lot and his uncle, though we see Abraham's love for Lot to the very last scene, when he surveys the smoldering ruins of Sodom and Gomorrah.

And even though he didn't need to blame himself, he probably did. Because that's what we do, as parents, friends, family members, coworkers. We wish we could have done more. Wish the story ended differently. Wish rehab or jail or detention or community service or whatever corrective measures Lot had, had worked.

But ultimately, we can say with Abraham, "Will not the Judge of all the earth do right?" (Gen. 18:25). We know this about Lot, and about the Lots in our world. We know that God loves our Lots. And about that, we carry no regrets. Only gratitude.

TRAVELING MERCY
Dear one,
Perhaps you are Lot
Or you are Abraham
Loving Lot,
But sometimes
You have to let the whole lot go
And trust me.
Because believe me,
You are all Lot and Abraham to me,
And I will never stop interceding.
Make me the centerpiece of your life,
Love wisely,
And know this:
I will take care of you
And your Lots.

NOTE TO SELF
God will do right. Always.

APRIL 24

LOT'S LOT

> The men grasped [their] hands . . . and led them safely
> out of the city, for the LORD was merciful to them.
>
> —GENESIS 19:16

The story of Abraham's nephew Lot reads like a sordid tale from a national tattler magazine. It's not the subject of children's books or polite dinner conversation. To his credit, and ultimately discredit because it did him so little good, Lot had a strong advocate in his relative. Uncle Abraham went on record numerous times, helping him, interceding for him with God. He plucked Lot out of the frying pan, but still Lot seemed to race right back into the fire.

Lot's story also could read like a classic tale of enabling. His Uncle Abraham taught him everything he knew about traveling and earning a living. But Lot was the shiftless relative who never quite owned up to his own character defects and failures, and ended up living in Sodom, a town so evil that God planned to destroy it.

Abraham begged God not to destroy Sodom, because what if there were just fifty, or forty-five, or twenty righteous persons living there? Abraham pressed God even further: "What if only ten can be found there?" (Gen. 18:32).

God agreed and saved Lot (who may not have been one of the ten righteous people in the city) and his wife and daughters. The girls' fiancées grinned and gaped, and maybe guffawed, and said, "You're kidding? Really? You think God's gonna destroy this city? No way. We're staying." The family of four escaped, but Lot's wife, who sadly remains nameless, was a mess. She left with Lot, but looked back on the city with longing. God turned her into a little pile of salt in the desert. That's a sad lot and final plot in life.

Not only didn't Lot or his wife make the most of Abraham's intervention, but neither did the daughters. They participated in destructive, irresponsible behavior and lived without faith in the God who rescued them. As a result, they both had children who became enemies of God's people.

Uncle Abe's intercession with God spared Lot's life, but none of Lot's family learned the lesson of freedom. Freedom comes with a price: responsibility, living up to the life you've been offered.

Maybe your history reads like Lot's. It's not too late for God to rework your life trajectory. Lot didn't have to end up living holed up in a cave in a mountain, his family in ruins. Even from the cave, he could have turned to the God who saved him from destruction.

Or maybe you're Uncle Abraham and someone in your extended trove of relatives is Lot. You've done everything you can to help save your Lot and still, Lot just doesn't get it, doesn't respond by stepping into the life God could give him.

How did Abraham handle Lot's irresponsibility? He begged God to bail out Lot from the town burning with evil, and God did. But when Lot fled, Abraham could only entrust his relative into God's hands.

Which is all any of us can do. Entrust our loved ones to God, though we grieve their lot in life, that little spot they occupy with such striking finesse and bravado or else with complete capitulation.

Abraham loved as often as the opportunity arose, and we can do the same. Love. Pray. And keep walking on our own journeys toward God and God's promises. And who knows? Maybe our Lots will intersect with someone else, someone walking toward freedom, and our Lots will join the caravan.

TRAVELING MERCY
Dear one,
Come here, child.
You've tried so hard,
You've loved so well,
But sometimes you just have to entrust
Those you love to me.
Your journey is yours alone,
And the same is true for those you love.
But this you can hold tightly to:
I will always have Someone
To stand in the gap for your loved ones.
This does not all depend on you.
So trust me,
Keep loving,
Be wise, and
Keep walking.

NOTE TO SELF
Today, pray, trust, walk, and love.

APRIL 25

LOT'S WIFE'S FINAL PLOT

"Flee . . . ! Don't look back, and don't stop!"
—Genesis 19:17

There is a time for retrospect. A time for remembering, processing, and learning from our past. But right before the city became engulfed in flames? That was not that time.

Not for Lot, not for his wife, and not for their two daughters. The angels handcuffed their wrists and hauled them out of the doomed city. But somehow, in spite of the angels' words, "Flee for your lives! Don't look back, and don't stop anywhere on the plain!" Lot's wife still looked back.

Her past caught up with her and consumed her. Her longing for the life she needed to evacuate took up all her brain and thought. It latched on like a tail on a donkey, and she could no longer walk forward without one last long look at her past. She could only see the past parts of her life. Though the angels said, "Don't!" she couldn't resist. It was the death of her.

Haven't we known people who gave up smoking but every day for the rest of their lives the scent of cigarette smoke in their nostrils, the sulfur strike of a match, or the click of a lighter raised their hopes for just one more hit? Just one. Or the alcoholic who lives with a longing for a drink as constant and involuntary as breathing, in spite of years of sobriety? Or gamblers, whose hands always itch without the cold, smooth cubes of dice, their *clackety-clack* on the table, and the thrilling rush of risk shooting like adrenaline through their veins?

But even if we haven't left behind an addiction or an unhealthy relationship, we have walked away with regrets, and we lug with us the longing to have behaved differently, to have acted with more wisdom or maturity. To have been different people when faced with the those circumstances. Maybe our lives would have turned out differently then.

Is our longing for the past unlike Lot's wife's desire? Just because our brains know that we've had to walk out or walk away so we could walk on, doesn't mean that our heart and soul followed the trail. Lot's wife left, but her heart stayed behind. And it destroyed her.

Sometimes we need to log some miles before we can look behind us with any clarity. Or safety, for that matter. We flee with the clothes on our back and hopefully our loved ones by our sides. We flee to the mountains, to a safe place, and from there, when we've caught our breath and the stitch in our side becomes a memory, we can process our journey.

Granted, if we don't process it, our past and our pleasures and our pain will rule us. But if we look back too soon, we might get swept away. Like Lot's wife, whose final plot was a piece of land the size of her feet.

Fast-forward now, rewind later. Flee for your lives. In the heat of the moment, heed the angels' warning.

TRAVELING MERCY
Dear one,
Your past is behind you,
And of course you have regrets
And maybe even still longings
For the land you've fled,
Because you are, well, human.
But if every incident
Directs you toward me
Then isn't it worth it all?
That's the goal.
But please
Rest first then reflect;
Learn from the looking back.
It's the best way around regret,
And the best way
To become yourself
As I know you.
It's the only route
Toward freedom.

NOTE TO SELF
Live today, long for tomorrow.

APRIL 26

A NO-SALT DIET

"Flee there quickly, because I cannot do
anything until you reach it."

—Genesis 19:22

Aren't we like Lot and his wife, pining for old loves, lost loves, bad loves, good loves? Whether it was the riches, the lifestyle, the hedonism, the company she kept, Mrs. Lot couldn't leave it behind. How easy to make idols of our past, without any perspective on its costly damage to us and our loved ones.

But we also live in the land of look-back when it comes to our "wish-I-would-haves" or "wish-I-wouldn't-haves." Regrets, griefs, and also legitimately happier times will give us a crick in our necks.

If we don't eventually reread and study those past pages, we won't learn from our lives. To pretend that it is all behind us— God has saved us, after all! Just move on—without processing those chapters leaves us unfinished, unformed people strewn like bodies in an accident. Such litter our families, our churches, our friendships. But mostly that's us. People who never become.

Without candid evaluation, we won't know how to make different choices, how to proceed with wisdom. We won't discover the takeaway value. But this requires perspective, distance, time. Sometimes it's just too soon. The smoke still rises from our destroyed past. The dust plumes from our desert run away from the destruction. We can still smell the burning pitch.

How do we remember the past and still trust God for the future? How do we keep living fully in today, in the almost-not-quite days of our lives?

A lot of recovery can happen with lists. Lists of significant memories, including the regrets and the stupid decisions. But as part of the list, we have to include what the items cost us and what we learned from them. Then, our memories and past lose some of their fearsome power over us. Nothing like pen and paper to help us see the reality and to "become" from it.

And then, what if our life moments and memories, those big and little losses or colossal mistakes that dominate our minds at the most minute reminders—the smell of a campfire, for instance, might do it in Lot's case—act as a mirror in a periscope? The mirror at the end of a periscope allows us to see at an angle and shows us what's outside our normal viewing range.

Life events become the mirror and bounce our vision up and out of our prairie dog hole or mountain keep, and up to God.

Then our memories don't trap us or decimate us. We don't have to live like we don't have a past; we can share the view with others. Rather than leaving us a pillar of salt on the desert floor, destroyed by looking back, our memories help us become an icon.

An icon always directs the viewer's gaze to God. To the God who saves, the God who calls, the God who promises.

TRAVELING MERCY

Dear one,
It's a costly journey,
And there is a time to tally the costs
And realize how much
This trip through life
Has cost you.
To make that list
Will help you leave the past behind,
To stop longing,
Stop regretting,
And start living forward once again.

NOTE TO SELF

Count the costs and profits and losses,
then start living.

APRIL 27

A TOWN CALLED SMALL

I lift up my eyes to the mountains—where does my help come from?
My help comes from the LORD, the Maker of heaven and earth.

—PSALM 121:1–2

When Lot fled from Sodom, his angel visitors ordered him to head for the mountain. He protested. "No, let me just run to this little town. I'll never make it to the mountain" (see Gen. 19). So the messengers agreed, and Lot undermined God's best. But upon arrival, Lot feared for his life in the small town, which historians named Zoar (meaning "small") and at last fled to the mountains.

What might have happened if he'd trusted God first? If he'd run first to the mountain getaway that God had planned for him, rather than lowering his sights to a tiny little bump in the road called Zoar? The Scriptures don't tell us why he was frightened. If he could see the wreck of Sodom and Gomorrah, the smoke from the ruins still smudging the sky with the soot of sin, that seems ample enough reason. Maybe, though, he just didn't want to break entirely with his past.

Ironic, however, that God wanted to give him a mountain getaway, and he settled on a hamlet describable only by its given name of Small. His small choice ultimately meant the demise of his family.

When God called my husband and me out of the local church pastorate and into a full-time, freelance, missionary-type existence, I spent hours every day sweating about income, worrying about making ends meet, and making phone calls. I knew how much I needed to earn as a writer and speaker to help keep the lights on and the fridge semi-full. I battled away through introductions on the telephone (which is sometimes like trying to slip through a coil of barbed wire) with groups in neighboring towns. I cried a lot and worry corroded my faith. It didn't help my family much either.

One day, I sat at my desk, piles of paper around me, the humidity index high and the temperature about 110 degrees (Fahrenheit, lest you worry), sweat seeping from my pores. When the phone rang, I pounced.

A sweet Southern voice drawled, "Jane Rubietta? We met last year, and I wondered if I could refer you when people invite me to speak?"

We chatted for some time, and I hung up the phone, trembling from the miracle of God's kindness. Minutes passed and the phone rang again. A missionary in Mexico wondered if I would want to lead a retreat at their English-speaking church. The only catch? It would be held in a mountaintop resort . . . in Mexico.

After the call, I burst into tears. I was working at a killing pace, just trying to get to the nearest town called Small so I could pay a little bill or two, and God was inviting me to get away to the mountains. In Mexico.

Unlike Lot, I said yes.

And the view from that mountain was unlike anything I'd ever seen—I stood on the balcony, breathing in the twinkling air, and savored the vista of starry night and bright blinking city with deep inky blackness behind. The next day, the clouds rolled in and covered the valley, leaving us cuddled and swathed. I felt like Moses, the mountain smoking with God's presence. The Lord did a sweeping work that weekend in women's lives.

But even more, in my life. Because, en route to freedom, Small doesn't mean safe. And it just may mean missing God's best.

TRAVELING MERCY
Dear one,
Lift up your eyes!
Don't focus on the small;
Focus on my very best,
And that might just be
The mountaintop you've missed.
But don't miss my love for you,
Don't miss my protection of you,
Don't miss my provision for you.
Because I am your Maker,
The creator of heaven and earth,
And the plans I have for you
Are anything but small.

NOTE TO SELF
Today, no small choices. Only yes to mountain adventures.

APRIL 28

A LONG-TERM REDEMPTION

[God] remembered Abraham, and he brought Lot out of the
catastrophe that overthrew the cities where Lot had lived.

—Genesis 19:29

Lot's story ends with such sadness and desperation. His daughters, isolated from their former party life in Sodom, bereft of their laughing but now dead fiancées, and their mother now a few salt crystals on the desert floor, sank into deep despair. No fiancées, no future, no children, no hope. They would die old maids, failures in the eyes of anyone they met.

They holed up in a cave on the side of a mountain, miserable, Lot terrified to stay in that town called Small. Then one of the daughters decided to get her father drunk, and plied him with wine so that she could have a child and continue the family line, because in their hole in the wall cave, there were evidently no suitable men coming to call. The next day, it seemed like such a brilliant idea that she convinced her sister to do the same.

It hurts my heart to even read this again, because Abraham tried so hard to redeem Lot and fought for his life repeatedly. The angels got in on the job even. But Lot's past was stickier than the tar pits around Sodom and Gomorrah, and he just couldn't leave the past alone.

A LONG-TERM REDEMPTION

And neither could his girls.

They both conceived children, born of their father. The older daughter gave birth to a son, and she called him Moab, which sadly sounds like the Hebrew word for "from father." Her sister's son was called Ben-Ammi, meaning, "son of my people." The Moabites and the Ammonites would be considered the Hebrew people's enemies for generations to come. Abraham's offspring were forbidden to intermarry with Lot's descendants, and though related through Lot to Abraham, they were considered foreigners.

And then, surprise of all surprises, many years later, we meet up with a woman named Ruth, a Moabitess, who married an Israelite, the son of Naomi. Ruth gave up her false religion and became her mother-in-law's caregiver when the men of the family starved to death in a famine. "Your people will be my people," she declared, "and your God my God" (Ruth 1:16).

Ruth would care for this woman who'd endured sweeping grief and loss, would take Naomi back home to Bethlehem, and would marry a man named Boaz. The newlyweds would give birth to a son, named Obed, who would have a baby named Jesse, who would have a son named David, who would become the king of Israel. David would have a son who would have a son who would have a great-great-great grandson, and they would call his name Emmanuel, because he would save his people from their sin.

And God, after all those years, would bring hope full circle by including a Moabite in the family line of Jesus Christ. Imagine the smile on Abraham's face to know how *that* story turned out.

TRAVELING MERCY

Dear one,
You never know
The plans I have
To bring good from the pain
And beauty from the brokenness
And bounty from the barrenness.
Keep holding on to me,
Because my hope and plan
Is always to bring people
Into my grace.
Don't give up;
The best is coming.

NOTE TO SELF

Am I in this for the long haul?
Because God is the full circle God.

APRIL 29

REPEAT OFFENDER

> To Sarah [Abimelek] said, "I am giving your brother a thousand
> shekels of silver. This is to cover the offense against you
> before all who are with you; you are completely vindicated."
>
> —Genesis 20:16

Rarely is the journey to grace, to freedom, a straight line. Abraham and Sarah hiked onward, after the debacle of deceit in Egypt when Abraham told Pharaoh, "She's my sister, so sure, no problem, she can be your wife." God rescued Sarah, the one who would bear the heir, but Abraham didn't press ENTER on the takeaway. Years later in their travels, he passed off Sarah once again as his sister, and the king, smitten by her beauty, brought her into the palace.

Learning from our mistakes provides a sure-footed path on the journey to freedom, if we allow our past to instruct us. Unfortunately, that trail crumbled a bit with Abraham, it seems, when it came to Sarah.

At least this new king, Abimelek, had a tuning fork for his conscience, even if Abraham didn't. God spoke to the king in a dream. "You are as good as dead because of the woman you have taken; she is a married woman" (Gen. 20:3). Good as dead. There's a legacy. Turns out that God rendered Abimelek, his wife, and his slave girls incapable of bearing children on account of Sarah. Thus would end that king's family line. The text doesn't tell us how long this went on, but long enough for them to know they were barren. So perhaps a couple of months passed, at least, while Sarah was stuck in yet another king's harem.

"Don't mess with God's anointed" seems to be the message. I read this passage and take comfort. People will try to interfere or meddle or muddy the waters around us. Things will go wrong and problems will erupt like geysers. Betrayals happen. That's a promise from this broken world. But God can do anything. "You're as good as dead," God said to the king, and now to anyone who messes with God's children. With you and your loved ones. With me and mine.

But sadly, this latest mess didn't start with the king. (He wasn't wife-stealing as far as he knew, though taking a woman in addition to his wife could be considered greedy, I suppose. Wanting what isn't ours leads us into a dangerous trap. And the Ten Commandments hadn't been given yet.) Abraham's half-truth veiled the deeper issue.

This latest installment of Sarah's saga still seems to result from her husband's fear. I would be speechless with rage, if I were Sarah. No, not speechless, not for long. I would be spewing vitriol, an absolute fountain of angry words. Especially since this was a repeat offense. But even more outrageous is that Abraham's cowardice occurred after the angels' visit at Mamre, after the promise of a baby within a year.

Before we repeatedly smack our foreheads over Abraham's seeming lack of faith in the God who promised him a world full of descendents, maybe we'd better ask: What do we get from this excerpt in Sarah's saga? People will betray us, but God still speaks into dreams, into circumstances, into our very lives. And people's betrayal, whether caused by fear, lack of faith, or any other root, does not nullify God's promises.

People do not get the last word in this trek toward our promise. God does. Didn't King Abimelek say, "You are completely vindicated" to Sarah? And the next chapter in Sarah's saga begins, "Now the LORD was gracious to Sarah, as he said . . ."

Just so, the Lord will be gracious to us, as well. No matter the betrayal, the fear, the lack of faith. God will be gracious. So we hold tight to that promise on this long, treacherous walk toward freedom.

TRAVELING MERCY

Dear one,
My heart hurts at the pain
You endure over others' betrayal,
Over fear operating in their lives.
But you have a choice
At this juncture,
A choice that points you
Either in the direction of freedom
Or of enslavement.
You can decide
Whom you will trust.
Am I not the God who promised,
The God who still speaks,
The God who delivers
On all my promises?
I will lead you into freedom
Though it be a costly journey
For you
And for me.

You have been devalued and even debased.
But bringing you to freedom
Cost me my Son.
So I have every intention of making good
On my promise.
Come along, now.
I will be gracious to you.

NOTE TO SELF
God's promises get the last word.

APRIL 30

MORE THAN A THOUSAND

"You are completely vindicated."
—Genesis 20:16

From Abraham's tent, he surveyed the burning pit that once was Sodom and Gomorrah, the land of his nephew Lot's inheritance (Gen. 19:27–28). He shook his gray head at the destruction, and surely his heart grayed as well, grieving the losses of his closest relative. Lot's entire life, his possessions, everything he'd presumably held dear, including his wife, gone. All that remained of Lot's big dreams and his myopic existence was a charred plot of land, and a zip code outside of a town called Small.

Abraham turned, packed his bags, and relocated. Again. Someplace away from the pain, where he couldn't see the remains of his nephew's burned-out dreams. He bundled up his belongings, his throat taut with grief, and sojourned in Gerar. We've chased our tails around this barn before. Maybe not literally, but here again Abraham walked around in circles morally.

At the border of Gerar (which means, conveniently, "circle"), he pulled Sarah aside and whispered, "Pretend you are my sister." He didn't even bother to tell her how beautiful she was this time, like he had at the hemline of Egypt. Just, "Pretend. It will save my hide." He put out the word when questioned and pressed for introductions. "And meet Sarah, my dear, sweet, lovely sister." He patted her back amiably, just like a brother.

Sure enough, Abimelek the king sent for Sarah and took her into his elite inner circle. As Abraham's breath of fear gushed out in relief, did he stop to consider what God had promised? Not long before, hadn't God at last spelled out in detail the rest of the promise? "Your wife Sarah will give birth this time next year." Your *wife*, Abraham. The one with the new name, the one there behind the tent flap who just made sixty loaves of bread for your guests. Yes, that one. Remember?

He took an enormous risk sending Sarah off with King Abimelek. Sarah, now presumably no longer barren but ready to conceive at any moment.

Right about now, we could take a real dim view of this man, and no doubt Sarah did, too. But even though Abraham abandoned her into another's clutches and gave her up to another man's bed, God did not forsake her.

God closed the wombs of all the women in the household, then appeared in a dream to the king. "You are as good as dead because of the woman you have taken; she is a married woman" (Gen. 20:3).

God and the king did right by Sarah. The king addressed her directly, one of the few times we see anyone speak to her in her storyline. "I am giving your brother a thousand shekels of silver. This is to cover the offense against you before all who are with you; you are completely vindicated" (Gen. 20:16).

Hear this story, then consider the risks to the promise and the progeny, the risks to the marriage. But what about the risks to Sarah? She would be considered damaged goods and despised for the rest of her life. But the king rose above Abraham's lies and half-truths and selfishness and proved himself to be a man who feared God and honored Sarah.

Sarah could walk out of that palace with her head held high, dignity intact. "You are completely vindicated."

And we, too, can walk forward with our heads held high. No matter the places where shame and pain have taken us. God, our merciful God, completely vindicates us. We are completely vindicated through the One who would come, hundreds of years later, from Sarah's line. Vindicated, at the cost of his life.

TRAVELING MERCY

Dear one,
You, too, are completely vindicated.
Refuse now
To live in the past pain
And the shame
And rather to live
In the reality
That you have been bought with a price.
Your shame is gone.
You are free.
Completely vindicated.

NOTE TO SELF
Record expunged. Live free.

MAY DEVOTIONS

MAY 1

GOD OF THE IMPERFECT

God healed Abimelek, his wife and his female slaves
so they could have children again.

—Genesis 20:17

For the patriarch of a large clan, a godly man, Abraham sure pulled some boneheaded moves. The double foul with Sarah, first in Egypt and then with King Abimelek, ranks high on the list of hazardous behavior. But in the clench, under fire by the king who had Sarah under his wing, Abraham lost all discretion and tact.

Furious at the deception, the king roared at Abraham, "What have you done to us? How have I wronged you that you have brought such great guilt upon me and my kingdom? You have done things to me that should never be done" (Gen. 20:9). He pressed Abraham for an explanation, and here's where the king wins points for self-control and Abraham loses a few.

"There is no fear of God in this place," Abraham said. *Gulp*. He should've swallowed his tongue right then. Really? This, to the ruler who had listened to God and obeyed instantly? Who demonstrated great fear of God in the presence of apparent wrongdoing and immediately set the matter right?

Abraham, Abraham. Is this senility or just a temporary lack of mental clarity? Or more likely a mind buzzed on fear?

Then Abraham wandered through an explanation, about a stepmother and offspring, and to the king's credit, he still forgave Abraham and, get this, blessed him with still more sheep and cattle and slaves. Why?

Because, after appearing in Abimelek's dream and clearing him of any wrongdoing, God said, "Now return the man's wife, for he is a prophet, and he will pray for you and you will live" (Gen. 20:7). This is the first place Scripture uses the word *prophet*—a prophet, mind you, proven to be both coward and liar. But Abimelek feared God and trusted him for the healing of the king's family and slaves.

And ultimately, he trusted God's assessment of the man who refused to stand in the gap for his own wife. He trusted Abraham to stand in the gap for him, that he and his household might be healed. The king trusted. Abraham prayed. God healed.

There we have it. God didn't select a perfect man from the ranks of the world class to be the founder of a great nation—there were none in the database. God chose a human being, full of fear and hope and grief and laughter. And began the process of conversion.

Isn't that the way for us, as well? Imperfect, riddled with pain and pockmarked with our own personal cowardices and fears, longings and losses. God calls us, just like Abraham, to bless. And to grow. And to bless again.

But that's not all, is it? We, too, like King Abimelek, begin to trust God to work through the imperfect people in our lives. Because that's the only choice we have.

TRAVELING MERCY
Dear one,
It's just perfect;
And that's the reason
It's a miracle.
Because no one is perfect
Except for me.
So anytime
People act imperfectly,
I get to show my hand
And bless.
So expect blessing,
But also
Don't let your fear
Run and ruin
Your life or the lives
Of people you love.
Trust me,
Come to me,
And you will see.
Just watch.

NOTE TO SELF
Love imperfectly but love anyway.

MAY 2

STANDING IN THE GAP

Then Abraham prayed to God.
—Genesis 20:17

In spite of missteps and flat-out mistakes, Abraham was not afraid to go before God and plead. He stood in the gap time and again. What a hallmark of his faith.

He interceded for Lot by going to battle for him after Lot's capture by the marauding kings (Gen. 14).

He interceded for Ishmael. When God changed Sarai's name to Sarah and promised a child through her, Abraham begged God, "If only Ishmael might live under your blessing!" (Gen. 17:18).

He interceded for Lot before the destruction of Sodom and Gomorrah, bargaining with God to save any righteous people. There he prevailed upon God's righteousness and justice: "Far be it from you to do such a thing—to kill the righteous with the wicked, treating the righteous and the wicked alike. Far be it from you! Will not the Judge of all the earth do right?" (Gen. 18:25).

And God assumed the best of Abraham, calling him up to the next important intercession. When Abraham messed up in Gerar, God appeared to King Abimelek in the dream and said of Abraham. "He is a prophet, and he will pray for you and you will live" (Gen. 20:7). But if the king didn't return Sarah to Abraham, God absolutely guaranteed him that he and all of his people would die.

That's some powerful motivation. And once Abraham had his wife back in his arms, the Scriptures tell us, "then Abraham prayed to God, and God healed Abimelek, his wife and his slave girls so that they could have children again" (Gen. 20:17).

Age never deterred Abraham when it came to adventure, and standing in the gap is a powerful means of blessing others, regardless of age or health or mobility. Whether we're young or old, whether we're running marathons or gripping the handles of a walker, whether we live full tilt or are stretched out on our backs, we can pray. We can throw ourselves between God and others, physically, we go (cede) between (inter) two parties to attempt to reconcile, to bring the two sides together.

Intercession knows no boundaries. Ask Corrie ten Boom or Dietrich Bonhoeffer or the apostle Paul. Ask the people who pen letter after letter to leaders or editors, standing in the gap for others. Ask the foreign diplomats who press for the release of political prisoners and captives of war. Ask my great aunt Mae, who stood in the gap for my mother and for all our family for all our lives until she went to heaven in person. (She's probably still pulling on Jesus' elbow about us.) Ask the people whose rooms glow with God's presence, little rooms in nursing homes and prison cells and convalescent centers and convents and closets that are converted to prayer altars. Ask the people who approach the bench of the great God on high.

Ask Jesus, who "always lives to intercede" for us (Heb. 7:25).

Whether we are flat on our backs or flattening our palms on the floor, we, too, get to live to make intercession. To stand in the gap. No more barrenness then. Just bounty.

TRAVELING MERCY
Dear one,
I hear your prayers
No matter where you are.
And while we're at it,
Know that my Son
Always stands in the gap for you,
Right now,
Last week,
Next year,
Always.
And how I delight to see you
There in the gap
For others.
It's a perfect circle of
Blessing and blessed
And blessing again.

NOTE TO SELF
Happy to be the go-between.

MAY 3

DESERT DECISIONS

> Now the Lord was gracious to Sarah, as he had said,
> and the Lord did for Sarah what he had promised.
>
> —Genesis 21:1

She was so old. She'd waited a very long lifetime for God to make good on that promise to her husband. She'd followed that man from pillar to post. Abraham was seventy-five when God called him, and when at last the three visitors made their announcement in Genesis 18, he was ninety-nine. Sarah endured humiliation and abandonment from his hand, however culturally accepted or expected his actions might have been. She'd been the barren one, the unfulfilled one, the defective one. And haven't we all, in some measure, experienced the same? And haven't we all, throughout our lifetime, be it long or short, been challenged to keep trusting the One we can't see, even though the one we can see and are tempted to trust is so . . . human?

Maybe it's precisely because we are all so human, so failure-prone, that we long for a promise greater than ourselves, greater than the word and witness of those around us. Because, when we scan the skyline of our lives, we pinpoint the problems and pain, and this vision becomes its own prison.

In that era, leaving Abraham because of his foibles and seeming mistakes would have been nearly impossible. How would Sarah survive? Even though kings had given Abraham money on her behalf, she'd have left as an impoverished woman because women likely couldn't own property. So leaving wasn't an option, at least, not a viable option.

Or, she could have made Abraham's life miserable and dragged the past into the present, marring every moment together with her rants. Maybe she did. Maybe she had a real mouth in the middle of her beautiful face, and spoke only the language of ugly. That's not, however, the picture we get of her, because when we act ugly, it's often based in our fears, and Sarah is recounted as a woman who did not give in to fear (see 1 Pet. 3:6).

No, she looked beyond her relationship with her spouse, to the horizon of God's promises. And month after month, while she waited, she managed to stay focused on that promise. "You'll have more children than stars in the sky, than sand in the desert." (There are more grains of sand in a cubic foot than there are people alive in the world, so that's quite a promise God made. One of hyperbole, we assume, but so rich and dense.)

Every time she flipped the monthly calendar to the next sheet, she had to choose: fear or faith? And she kept walking. Surely, given all the tumultuous events in their journey, Sarah and Abraham needed time to heal, time to come back together as a couple, time to have a history and a story and a relationship. Then, at just the right time, God fulfilled the promise to Sarah, and her withered womb quickened with life.

Isn't this so for us, as well, as we wait for our heart's desire, as we wait and pray and weep and gnash our teeth and pace and worry and try to connive our way through to the fulfillment of that desire? Ultimately, it comes down to God's promise and God's timing. And all the God-sightings en route only serve to strengthen our faith, to bind us together with the people we love, and to help us wait. Not always patiently. Not always lovingly. But we wait.

We trust. And in the fullness of time, God answers. God delights to deliver on his promises. So run to the window and scan the sky. At any moment, God may be answering your greatest plea. You'll want to be there when it happens.

TRAVELING MERCY
Dear one,
Keep watching for me
For I am en route,
Special delivery.
The desires of your heart
Are not forgotten.
They are, in fact,
Engraved on my own heart.
And so I, too, wait
And watch for the perfect timing,
The perfect setting in your heart,
The perfect moment
To fulfill my desires for you.
Keep watching.
I'm on the way.
And I want you to recognize me
When you see me.

Meanwhile, don't let the imperfects
In your life
Turn you from me.
I'm loving you through them,
And others through you,
And one day
It will all make sense.
Because . . .
I love you.

NOTE TO SELF
Fear won't steal my faith in God.

MAY 4

THE VISIT THAT CHANGED THE WORLD

The LORD visited Sarah just as he had said he would.
—GENESIS 21:1 NET

After that embarrassment at the tent, when Sarah laughed behind the doorway and God caught her, she sometimes wondered if she'd blown her chance at being part of the fulfillment of that promise. Especially since they'd had such a terrible year after that. Talk about the dark before the dawn. Lot's disastrous turn of events, his wife, his daughters. Abraham passing off Sarah to King Abimelek. That turned out OK, but you never know. Good thing God struck the whole palace with the catastrophe of barrenness. That sure got—or redirected—the king's attention.

Isn't that one of the amazing things about God? In spite of all that turmoil, in spite of Sarah's laughter, God rescued her. God sent the disaster on the king to protect *her*. She'd never realized that God cared about her in such a protective and proactive way.

So God visited her—and this is the first time God really visited Sarah. Always before, God was with Abraham and she was standing off in the shadows or in the background or asleep in bed or baking bread (or nagging Hagar). But now, God visited her—little, old, tired, tired-of-waiting, and not-always-gracious Sarah. The word *visited* is translated in some versions of Scripture as "Now the Lord was gracious to Sarah," but the Hebrew language actually uses the word *visit*.

And that word *visit* indicates a special attention, sometimes for the purpose of divine intervention of blessing or cursing. God's visit, this kind of visit, always changes the life of the one visited. Whether God is visiting the Amalekites, for instance, with destruction, or visiting the Israelite people in Egypt to rescue them, God's visits always change lives.

This visit would be no different, and Sarah's life would change as dramatically as anyone's life in all the stories to follow. "Sarah became pregnant and bore a son to Abraham in his old age, at the very time God had promised him. Abraham gave the name Isaac to the son Sarah bore him" (Gen. 21:2–3). From this double confirmation, the text makes it absolutely clear that when God visited, Sarah bore Abraham a son, a son who came from both of them, a son who was absolutely *their* son and no doubt about it. And the ripple effect of change began, and continued, and the waves roll right up to our shoreline, and lap at the ankles of our faith.

About those visits. What if they happen like that today, for us, as well? What if, every time we visit with God and God visits with us, it changes our lives? What if we visit with God expecting to be changed? To be filled with God's presence, God's holiness, God's love, the fruit that comes from such a visit?

Wouldn't that change our lives? Wouldn't that change the lives of all the people in our lives?

Wouldn't that, in fact, change the world? God visits and changes our destinies. And changes the world.

That works for me. So today, in moments of deliberate seeking of God and in moments of fast-forward, rush hour style living, and even in the moments (make that, hours) when I'm on hold with various tech providers, I'll watch for that. Imagine that. A visit that changes the world.

I think the world needs a divine visit. And so do we.

TRAVELING MERCY
Dear one,
Whether you were behind the door laughing
Or waiting in the opening
I am still here,
And never left
And never will leave.
So if you have time
I have time
For a visit.
I always have time
For you.

NOTE TO SELF
Today I have time for a visit that changes the world.

MAY 5

A BELLYFUL

> "God has brought me laughter, and everyone who
> hears about this will laugh with me."
>
> —Genesis 21:6

What an impossible premise, the stuff of jokes—and dirty ones at that. "Ancient woman gets pregnant by antique husband!" the tabloids tattle. How could this even be? When the Lord told Abraham about the pending promise's fulfillment, Abraham laughed. Whether in disbelief or in delighted acceptance of the promised child, we aren't told, but ultimately it was an acceptance credited to him as "putting all things right."

When the angels from the Promise Fulfillment Center at Mamre first announced to Sarah, "One more year, and then, *voila*, it's 'dream come true' time," she, too, laughed. Maybe not in hilarity or joy or with delighted acceptance. But in scorn: "Really? *Moi*? Pregnant? You're kidding, aren't you? Not funny, oh trio of guests. So not funny. Your bad joke is just too late."

One visitor, who turned out to be God, called her on her laugh of disbelief. Yet the promise, the one that dovetailed perfectly with the one given to Abraham—that she would give birth to a son "this time next year"—proved true. Sarah's disbelief and disillusionment did not hinder that fulfillment—something to consider in our own waiting lives, while we keep hoping that the promises are still gestating in God's heart and mind. Though it sure seems like a record-breaking gestation, longer than an elephant's.

When the promised baby pushed his way into the world, when the naming ceremony took place, Sarah laughed. She laughed a pure, clear trill of joy and happiness.

When Abraham put his hand on the infant's crown and blessed him, he named him Isaac.

Laughter.

The rolling, stomach-tightening, heart-lifting blessing of laughter. Sarah said in response, "God has brought me laughter."

Laughter. What a healing gift. Not just the gift of a child, but after all the grimfaced wandering and wondering, after all the pain and disillusionment, laughter. Full, overflowing, free.

And laughter is such a contagious gift—don't they say, "Laugh and the world laughs with you"? (Forget the ending of that little couplet, for now.) Sometimes when I'm speaking, the audience and I get tickled. Laughter becomes airborne, viral, in the room. Often we laugh until tears leak from the corners of our eyes.

Laughter is like a heart replacement. It shifts our focus, massages our inner organs, lifts depression. Many doctors believe that laughter heals physical problems, and research and documentation back up their belief.

Life is hard, and then you die. Well, duh. Obviously. But somewhere along the way, we learn to break the hard-packed dirt of life and disappointment with the tines of laughter, planting seeds of joy as we sally forth. We have to find the funny in daily life. I love reading joke books, funny authors, and the quips in *Reader's Digest*. We watch funny movies (and I realize that they are funnier in others' presence) and tell each other jokes and stories.

And here, after all the years of chasing the promise, God's promise, Sarah and Abraham are given the gift of laughter. Healing laughter. But they don't keep it to themselves. No, they share the joy. They name their little bundle "Laughter," and Isaac forever after has the privilege of living into such a wonderful name.

Maybe we can make that our honorary middle name. May we live into God's promise through Isaiah, that "joy and gladness be found in [us], thanksgiving and the sound of singing" (Isa. 51:3).

TRAVELING MERCY
Dear one,
You've waited so long,
And yes, you've been troubled,
Impatient,
And just a wee bit disbelieving.
You've endured scorn and disappointment,
But you've endured;
You've lived.
Now let your tears turn to laughter
For the promise waits in your arms.
Lift up your heart to me,
For at just the right time
You will see.
I promise.

And I long to hear you laugh
The unhindered rolling laugh,
The deep belly laugh,
Of a happy child.

NOTE TO SELF
I will find the funny in my life today.

MAY 6

TIMING IS EVERYTHING

> Now the Lord was gracious to Sarah.
>
> —Genesis 21:1

Couldn't Sarah have quit a long time ago and given up on this God she barely knew but who had disrupted her entire life? She'd waited twenty-five years and been abandoned out on some steep ledges as she waited on God's grace to place a baby in her arms. She'd endured scorn and society's judgment and lived in a fragile marriage. She'd put up with her husband's nephew, who stayed around until reviewing the plot map and then grabbed a deed to the greenest land. She'd been ignored, deserted, hurt, judged, and grown old in the process.

How easy to give up. To assume that because things don't happen on our timetable that (a) they won't happen at all, (b) God doesn't have our best interests at heart after all, and (c) God actually isn't all that gracious . . . not to us, anyway. We can see God's graciousness in other people's lives—look at the Joneses, with their new car and great job and perfect children. Look at our colleagues, always getting the promotion and the favor. But about those promises we've been waiting on . . . not so much.

Isn't it easy to see God's grace operating in such overflowing ways in others' lives and to decide that clearly God has it out for us, or just forgot about us, or decided on a different plan but didn't bother to clue us in?

Our timing is so finite and our vantage point a pinhole compared to God's wide-angle lens. Our view of the world and the order of events is so restricted. Our gaze is so inward focused. We can't see behind the front door of the neighbor's home; we don't know the downside of that mogul's cush job, and we have no idea the costs accompanying what appears to be God's favor to others. Just because they're lounging in first-class, extra-wide leather seats and we're jammed back by the toilets with our knees up to our chins, doesn't mean that God isn't God or God isn't gracious to *us* or God doesn't care about us.

And those others, who always bubble over with praise about how God answered this prayer and solved that problem and took care of that issue and healed so-and-so, like those people laughing with the baby on their lap. . . . We cannot compare God's apparent graciousness to others and then scrap all of our dreams and God's promises to us, only to live a life of barrenness, a life unfulfilled and unfocused. We cannot sneak away or fritter away our days, abandoning our belief in God because God didn't act the way we thought he should act. The jaws of that trap are sharp and unforgiving.

But we need to listen to what our soul whispers to us as we peek out of our pinhole and notice other people's lives.

Disappointment in God is a key reason people walk away from church, or leave their childhood belief, or abandon their adult-sized faith. Shall we hold on to child-sized belief in God or begin to build our faith, to grow in our understanding of God and how God actually works?

Though we might not see it, can't explain it, or don't receive it, God is gracious. And we are all Abraham and Sarah, created and called by God. May we have the grace to recognize God's blessing and to live in that bounty.

TRAVELING MERCY
Dear one,
If you could explain me
Where would be
The mystery?
And if you could explain me
How would you live in faith?
But explaining me
And trusting me
Can be an oxymoron.
There are a few things
That you have to know, though:
I love you,
I'd do anything for you,
I know exactly the right time for that,
And finally,
I am gracious.
Don't let your disappointment
Keep you from seeking me
And finding me.
I promise
I will let you find me.

NOTE TO SELF
Notice disappointment and trust God anyway.

MAY 7

THE ONE WHO LAUGHS, LASTS

"God has brought me laughter."
—GENESIS 21:6

After a pretty grim quarter-century ride with her husband on the roller coaster of nomadic life, Sarah's teeth might have been ground down to stubs. Her dentist probably diagnosed her with TMJ and her internist prescribed therapy for carpal tunnel syndrome. Her hands probably still ached after baking sixty loaves of bread for the three guests the year before, when they'd changed her name and changed the course of her life and changed her body. She'd sure had a white-knuckle ride, given the Genesis overview.

But on this day, the whole world turned over in wonder for Sarah, and the earth awoke to the sounds of her delight. In her arms lay the promised child, and over this infant she laughed until she wept tears of joy. She wept until she laughed again, and Abraham came to her side and peered into the scrunched up little face, and he, too, laughed.

And the midwife looked up from her perch and a smile broke across her face, then a soft chuckle rolled out. The servants stood outside the tent flaps, gripping each other's hands and praying for mercy and waiting for the word of this long-awaited child's safe birth. When the groans of labor turned into cheers of laughter, they, too, burst out and laughed until they held their sides.

Even though experts say babies don't smile, surely not newborns, this baby surely laughed right back into his parents' faces, waving his fists at his new freedom and the sounds of joy flowing about him.

She would name him Isaac, meaning laughter, and laughter would be a sign of God's presence, of healing, of joy, for the rest of created time. Women and men forevermore would see laughter as a symbol of faith and "laugh at the days to come" (Prov. 31:25), as they put their hope in the God who brings barren wombs to life and allows an aged couple to give birth to a son who would give birth to sons who would give birth to sons who would one day become an entire nation, a nation that would bless the world. And those people who would end up in captivity back in Abraham's homeland would one day sing, "Our mouths were filled with laughter" (Ps. 126:2).

And one day, from the woman who laughed first in disbelief as she hid behind the tent flaps then laughed in overwhelming joy as she beheld the promised child, from this woman would come the One who would convert tears to joy and weeping to laughter, in the amazing heavenly acts of the God who came to earth.

Though people would laugh at him in disbelief, this same Man would offer astounding hope to the people who would listen: "Blessed are you who weep now, for you will laugh" (Luke 6:21).

We'd better strengthen our funny bones, because laughter is a sign of the kingdom.

TRAVELING MERCY
Dear one,
If only you could
Laugh more
And worry less,
And hold your sides
In joy
Rather than fear.
One day
You will be filled
With laughter,
And the world will laugh,
And gladness will ring
About the universe,
The laughter of a people
Well loved
Who lived well,
Who learned
To laugh
For God's sake.

NOTE TO SELF
Ask God to convert weeping to laughter. Starting now.

MAY 8

PARTY TIME

> The child grew and was weaned, and on the day
> Isaac was weaned Abraham held a great feast.
>
> —GENESIS 21:8

"The days crawl and the years fly" could be the slogan for parenting. These are the long, arduous, puzzling days when you recognize that you have no answers and are too exhausted to find any, and the endless nights of no sleep and little sleep and a lot of crying (both the parents' and the child's), and you think you are living out the movie *Groundhog Day*. But in the flash of a hummingbird's wing, years have passed.

In Abraham and Sarah's journey to freedom, only a header separates the story of Isaac's birth, the advent of the infant called Laughter, and his weaning. In reality, it was likely several years before Sarah weaned Isaac from her breast and began the detachment process.

Bring out the streamers and balloons, the chocolate cake and ice cream. Abraham threw a celebration for Isaac's move toward independence. For a child to be born to such elderly parents is miraculous, of course. But in an era of extremely high infant mortality, for a child to survive to be weaned was also miraculous. And so Abraham hosted a party.

Parties are good. We celebrate too seldom in our society, at least when it comes to honest celebrations rather than mere occasions to overindulge or to forget our troubles with mind-altering substances or other bingeing. But celebrating requires a certain focus, a choice to zero-in on the good, finding the joy-needle in a haystack full of troubles. For many of us, those slivers of joy remain elusive.

One friend, who'd seen her share of suffering and likely more coming down the pike since that's the way life works, often showed up with cappuccinos for the two of us, fresh from her own machine, and we made a party of the few minutes together, sitting on the stoop with the parade of people and cars passing by. Another, who steadfastly refused to acknowledge her hand in this, hung May Day flowers on our doorknob every single year. I have friends who celebrate the first day of spring, the first robin, the first day of summer, the smell of autumn, the first snow, and Thanksgiving leftovers.

Once I hosted a celebration dinner for our immediate little family, a statement of faith in a dissolved job prospect: God is faithful and has a plan, and this, evidently, is part of it.

Isn't a party a statement of faith, after all? That in the midst of darkness, we can celebrate because we have the Light of the World guiding our way? In Ecclesiastes 3:4, didn't even that sometimes-jaded agent of wisdom tell us there is "a time to weep and a time to laugh"?

Today, let's make a list. No, make two lists. One of all the weights we carry: the worries of the future and the problems and pain of our past. And another, all the ways we've seen God care for us.

Weighed on a scale, the God-list wins.

And then, bring out the balloons. God's care, even in—or especially in—or in spite of dark times, calls for a party. Maybe we can celebrate a weaning dependence on the world, and a growing dependence on the God who formed us and named us and calls us forward, always, toward freedom. It's our very own independence day and dependence day rolled into one.

TRAVELING MERCY
Dear one,
It's party time,
And I am celebrating,
Rejoicing,
Dancing over you,
Because I love you
And you are mine.
I shaped you in your mother's womb,
And everything in your life
Is intended to lead you to me.
So come;
Wean yourself from your worries
And depend on me.
Let's have a party;
I'm celebrating you.

NOTE TO SELF
Invite someone into a party today.

MAY 9

WORTH THE WILDERNESS

"Do not be afraid; God has heard."
—Genesis 21:17

The weaning party and choruses of joy ended on a sour note. Ishmael, by now a teen suffering from normal teenage angst, wasn't doing very well with the young "prince." Isaac came along and suddenly Ishmael's life turned upside down. Sure, his father loved him, but now Ishmael was just a tagalong, a half-relative in the dynasty, an illegitimate child with the DNA to prove it and nothing else. Sharing his father with Isaac proved to be too much for a kid struggling with identity issues and trying to figure out how to grow up.

So he laughed at Isaac during the blowout celebration, a teenage "I'm cool and you aren't" snort of derision. "It's not my party, but I can sure ruin it for you." Sarah, Ishmael's legal mother, but possibly not a loving one, heard and rose up in her primal mother fury and protectiveness of Isaac. She ordered Abraham to dispose of "that slave woman and her son" (Gen. 21:10).

Abraham took the problem to God (always a good idea). Only after hearing God's promise to take care of Ishmael did

Abraham comply, sending Hagar and Ishmael packing with a pathetic ration of water and a lunch box.

In the wilderness, their meager provisions depleted, Hagar shoved her limp, dehydrated son under a scrub bush. She dragged herself a hundred yards away, heartbroken, and sobbed. "I cannot watch the boy die."

And isn't this the way with us, sometimes? We land in the wilderness through no fault of our own. Then we watch the dehydration of all our hopes, the evaporation of our very spirit, the dying off of our promises and loved ones. We separate ourselves from our sources of deep pain and loss, from our anguish and our regret, from our anger at the people who have mistreated us. We shove our Ishmael under the brush and crawl away.

Hagar, brokenhearted and hopeless, thrown out into the wilderness and bewildered, probably felt betrayed by the God who once made a promise. During her pregnancy, God told her if she would only "return and submit," she would have descendants too numerous to count (see Gen. 16:9). And now look where it had gotten her and the child God named.

Without this void of abandonment and despair, Hagar—and we—would never know the reality of God's rescue and compassion, God's faithfulness to the promises.

The Scriptures say, "God heard the boy crying" (Gen. 21:17), though we have no other record of Ishmael's tears. But the God who hears broken hearts heard Ishmael. Heard Hagar. Heard, with the intent to rescue. God opened the slave woman's eyes to life-saving water nearby, a well. Ishmael, named "God hears" during Hagar's escape to the wilderness thirteen years ago, was now heard by God.

God does not turn a deaf ear to our cries. God does not forget the promises made to us in the wildernesses of our lives. God hears; God supplies.

Sometimes God just has to open our eyes. And without the wilderness, we might never see. But in the wilderness, we learn that the God who sees also hears and provides. Water in the wilderness. It is worth the trip.

TRAVELING MERCY
Dear one,
The wilderness
Forms you.
But even more than that,
It opens your ears
To your own heart
And your eyes to
My provision.
I see.
I hear.
I will supply.
Imagine that—
A well in the wilderness.
Who would think?
I would.
And one day
You will live in a place
Where you will never
Be thirsty
Again.

NOTE TO SELF
Watch for God's well in the wilderness.
It might be right around the bend.

MAY 10

REPUTATION AND RESPONSE

"No matter what you do, God is on your side."
—Genesis 21:22 msg

Abimelek surely shook his head in wonder. I mean, Abraham stayed there in Gerar even after his deceitfulness. Of course word traveled, and wasn't everyone interested in what happened to this man, Abraham? So Abimelek would know that right after he released Sarah from his household and invited Abraham to live wherever he wanted, that she became pregnant. Good thing the king gave Abraham the silver, so the watching world would know the child belonged to Abraham and not Abimelek. And what an unlikely story, what a—well, he would have to call it a miracle, right? Talk about a late bloomer. She was no child bride, not any longer. Nor was Abraham a virile young man. Virile, maybe, but young? No. They were both old, almost ancient by this time. Yes, a miracle.

So Abimelek shook his head in wonder and also a bit of disbelief. How did the old man do it? Not just manage to get Sarah pregnant, but to always come up in triumph, always with the blessing, always with things working out just right?

Abraham's reputation of courage and loyalty were legendary: giving the best piece of land to a high-rolling nephew, fighting kings and armies, blocking God's path to plead for that nephew's life. Word traveled. But the sketchy deal about Sarah, that was another story.

Still, after the unlikely miracle of that baby, the king sought out Abraham, knowing all about Abraham's courage and honor and his status as prophet. But he was also familiar with Abraham's shadiness, with his humanity. This is the wonder of his statement to Abraham: "No matter what you do, God is on your side." He knew both sides of Abraham and still watched God bless the foreigner.

Abimelek asked Abraham for reciprocity. Maybe he knew the promise, that promise that moved Abraham into King Abimelek's country in the first place—that God would bless him and make him a blessing. The king called in the chips and asked Abraham to hold to his end of the bargain: to be a blessing. "Swear to me that you won't do anything underhanded to me or any of my family. For as long as you live here, swear that you'll treat me and my land as I've treated you" (Gen. 21:23 MSG).

He called Abraham to integrity in the town whose name meant "circle." Called him back to the original promise.

So the king's words to Abraham serve as a testament to Abraham and to King Abimelek. But more than that, they are a testament to God. To the God who is always for us, for all of us, always hoping to redirect our hearts back to heaven. God, knowing our deceit, doesn't endorse it. Being "on our side" means God wants the best for us. And wants us to bless out of that best. And even, sometimes, out of our mess.

TRAVELING MERCY
Dear one,
I am always on your side.
I always want the best
For you,
For those you love,
Though that best
May not look like
You'd hoped.
But it's the truth.
I am always on your side,
Always seek your best.
And I want you to bless
In spite of any mess
Out of that best.

NOTE TO SELF
I've sure been a mess, but I can still bless.

MAY 11

TURN OF THE BLESSING WHEEL

"Through your offspring all peoples on earth will be blessed."
—Acts 3:25

After Christ's death and resurrection and his appearances to the Jewish believers, Peter preached to anyone who would listen anytime a crowd gathered. After Peter healed the crippled beggar, the crowd ran to hear what this man, who evidently worked miracles, could tell them. Even though our sin and shame hitchhike alongside, our hunger for life and miracle is nearly invincible.

Peter recounted the history of the Israelites, from Abraham through Moses and straight up to Jesus, and stated with bullhorn bluntness that they'd killed the author of life (see Acts 3:15), the very one through whom the world was to be blessed. To avoid a riot, he didn't stop there.

Peter restated the cycle of blessing, the inception of the blessing circle. There at Solomon's Colonnade, he cited God's promise to Abraham: "Through your offspring all peoples on earth will be blessed." Surely the people shuffled their feet, looked at the ground, and cleared their throats, cheeks red. Surely they felt the prick of guilt's sword as it pierced their hearts.

But again, Peter didn't leave them in their guilt. He restarted the cycle with hope (see Acts 3:26).

"When God raised up his servant [Jesus], he sent him first to you to bless you." Wait with that. After the people killed Jesus, God sent Jesus—Abraham's offspring!—back to those very people to bless them? But how, given the sin, the shame? Their separation from God? How, given our sin and our shame? Our separation from God?

"By turning each of you from your wicked ways" (Acts 3:26).

Turning us from our sin. The blessing wheel stops rotating when we sin. We dry out and split apart like empty rain barrels in desert heat.

But the wheel starts turning again when we repent. When we turn. Repentance isn't easy, but it is simple. And Peter said that God will do the turning. Can't you look back over the last day or week or month and find places where you separated yourself from God or from another person? Those are the places where we have stopped the blessing wheel. We start it turning again when we turn around and turn back to God and turn back to relationships.

And God's words, "You will be a blessing because I am blessing you," pour over us like a soft spring rain that soaks into our souls. "Repent, then, and turn to God, so that your sins may be wiped out, that times of refreshing may come from the Lord" (Acts 3:19). Blessing leads to repentance, which leads to blessing others.

Times of refreshing. Let the rains begin.

TRAVELING MERCY

Dear one,
Times of refreshing
Always come
With tears of repentance,
With acknowledgement of sin,
With the humility to say,
"I have messed up."
Then the barren desert
Of your soul
Will loosen,
And I will rain down love
From heaven,
And you will know
Times of refreshing.
Come.
Aren't you thirsty?

NOTE TO SELF

Turn to God. Turn around.
Turn the blessing wheel again.

MAY 12

TO THE HILT

After all this, God tested Abraham.
—Genesis 22:1 msg

After all this? After all the testing and trials and travels, Abraham got another test. The Jewish people reckon this to be about test number ten for Abraham. Surely he'd passed the exams already. Surely after all these years, God knew Abraham to be a faithful follower. A friend.

Had it really come down to this? First God asked him to part ways with his past. To leave, to go, to set out from Ur: "Go from your country, your people and your father's household" (Gen. 12:1). And now, fifty years later? "Go to the region of Moriah" (Gen. 22:2).

Now God was asking him to part ways with his future, with all his hopes for his future. To give it all up. The same word is used in the Hebrew for both commands from God: *Lekh-Lekha*. "Go, leave, separate from." In the first instance, Abraham parted company with the many gods of his household and his country and from all the ways of his past. And this time, God was asking him to go, to leave, to head to Moriah where he was to separate himself from his future, from his promised child, from such a source of joy and hope and the possibility of a great nation. *Lekh-Lekha*. Go, leave Ur. Go, leave your son.

That wasn't all. After all this, God was asking him to make this sacrifice, to respond in obedience, but didn't repeat the promise that had moved Abraham from Ur to Harran and through Canaan to Egypt and back again.

Perhaps Abraham left initially for the promise, but he stayed for the relationship, the remarkable reality and miracle of a relationship with this God, the mighty God, the one true God, the God who called him from barrenness into blessing. The God who blessed Abraham beyond all reason. But this time, God didn't reiterate the promise. And God was saying what, exactly? Break with your past, Abraham. And break with your future. And also, break with your dependence on my promises.

It's hard enough for us to break with the past, because even when we leave, the past follows us about like a loyal dog, panting at our heels. Leaving our past, whether yesterday or last year or a half-century ago, is a daily exercise.

But to break with our future? To give up tomorrow? Isn't that what people do when they are dying? That's not any way to live.

Or maybe it is the only way to live. Maybe that is the real question here: Are you willing to die to all your tomorrows, Abraham? Are you willing to put them to death, and live, right now, today? To live, really live, "Live entirely before me, live to the hilt!" (Gen. 17:1 MSG)?

Abraham didn't know how the ordeal would turn out. He didn't know that God would provide an alternate sacrifice. He didn't know that hundreds of years later, God's first commandment would be, "You shall have no other gods before me." That the most important rule ever would be, "Love the Lord your God with all your heart."

So he said, "Here I am," and readied himself for the hardest *today* of his life. This time, it felt like someone ripped his heart out of his chest. But he knew that the only way to live was to trust God right now.

And to know that tomorrow was in God's hands. And so it always will be.

TRAVELING MERCY
Dear one,
This is the hardest test
Ever.
I promise
That if you are willing
To break with your past
And break with your future
Then I will honor
Your heart
This day.
You have only today.
Today is yesterday's tomorrow
And tomorrow's yesterday.
It is the only time you have.
It's time to live
Today.

NOTE TO SELF
Let go of yesterday.
Release tomorrow.
That leaves today.

MAY 13

AVAILABLE

> "Here I am," [Abraham] replied.
> —Genesis 22:1

Abraham. A man mostly to be envied, except we're not supposed to covet. Plus, we might not appreciate a lot of elements about his life. Still, he was blessed beyond anything he could have hoped for: a beautiful wife, a treasured miracle child, material goods, favor with leaders and rulers. He would eventually be called a "friend of God," the first man in recorded history to bear that title. He of all people knew that he deserved no special treatment, no extra recognition, nothing.

After all these years, Abraham recognized God's voice, even though he came from a multiple-god home, city, and tradition. He knew this God. His soul chuckled with gladness over this God, over God's calling, over God's clear and abundant blessings. It was a miracle, and he knew it better than anyone.

So in the middle of the night, when he heard that voice calling through the dark, "Abraham!" he sat up in bed. He answered immediately.

"Here I am." Right here, God, ready for whatever you have in mind.

We see this with Samuel (1 Sam. 3:4), when God called him from his sleep. "Here I am." And again with Isaiah (Isa. 6:8), when God called him. "Here I am."

What we know about the next parts of these great leaders' stories is that life took a turn toward difficulty, stretching them at their yes to God. But none of them stopped to ask, "Wait, what will this cost me? What can I expect if I say yes to this?" They didn't back out of their yes, though hardship chased them.

Nor did Abraham. He woke up, sat up, stood up, and then bundled up his most precious promise, his son Isaac. The child he'd waited all his married life to hold. The child his dear wife would have a stroke about if anything happened to him. But he said yes and then stood in the middle of the absolute unknown, the vortex of impossible and crushing loss. Not knowing that absolute wonder, a miracle, would meet him on the mountain.

This sort of total, immediate, and radical obedience is born either of a deep encounter and experience with God, or a long relationship of knowing God, recognizing God's voice, and trusting God.

I would like that kind of reckless faith in God. Reckless, not because God impetuously demands reckless things of us. But reckless, because it forces us to loosen our grip on absolutely everything. Our loved ones. Our homes. Our stuff. Our dreams. Our expectations. Our hopes. Our future.

This answer, "Here I am," requires us to answer the question: Do we love the gift more than the Giver? Or the Giver more than the gift?

If we love the Giver more, then here we go. Wake up, sit up, stand up, and bundle up. The yes is the start of another great adventure. A hard one, perhaps. But one we will never regret. I like that. An open-handed, regret-free yes. Maybe it's the only way to stand in the middle of a miracle.

TRAVELING MERCY

Dear one,
No one said the word *easy*,
But it gets easier to say yes
The more you know me
And the more you live with me
And the more you follow me.
A yes means leaving
Your comfortable life
And bundling up your faith.
And it just starts with a simple
"Here I am."
And here's the good news:
Where you are,
I am too.
Because I am the I AM
Of Abraham.
And I am
The I AM
Of you.

NOTE TO SELF
Here I am.

MAY 14

TO LIVE LISTENING

"Yes?" answered Abraham. "I'm listening."
—GENESIS 22:1 MSG

Shhhhh. Do you hear it? The music on the air, in another's laugh, in the cadence of a voice or a baby's giggle. To live listening we have to throw away our ear buds and turn off the incessant background or foreground layer of sound. To tune in to the quiet, to the silence of snow falling or of trees dropping their skirt of leaves in a soft breeze.

If we aren't listening to the quiet we might never hear the sunrise, might not see the bird's first notes on its breath in the safety of daylight. We will be deaf to the carillon of stars in the summer sky or a deep winter's night with a moon sliver singing overhead.

We listen with our fingers, like a blind man feels faces. We listen, by touching. Another's hands, skin like an emery board or smooth as a newborn's cheek. We listen with our fingerprints, hearing another's soul by feeling their pulse. We hear people's actions rather than their words as we listen for their heart.

We listen with our eyes, with our nose, with our soul. We develop such keen hearing that we can hear the sound of God walking about in the garden in the cool of the day. We listen deeply, with practice. All our moments become moments of hearing God: God the artist painting the rim of the world with strokes of neon color. God the architect designing a dome over our universe more glorious than the Sistine Chapel. God the baker preparing sixty loaves of fresh bread for the visitors, thick and dense with steam rising like incense. God the perfumer testing the combinations for just the right scent of cut grass or pine trees or a skunk's spray or the heady aroma of a leaf of fresh basil.

We practice listening. For the weary breath beneath a person's smile, for the laughter outside the door. We listen for the twinkle in another's eye and feel the wind outside on the neighbor's chimes. For the sound of passing clouds and the school bus at the corner and running feet pattering down the hill.

We listen. And we begin to live. We live, and we learn to say yes, yes, many times yes. A lifetime of yes to God. To the God who designed, who dreamed, who created, who loves, who calls, who comes for us on the whisper and the shout, on the run and en route. We listen, and we learn to love, and to say, "Here I am." And we learn to live.

TRAVELING MERCY
Dear one,
It's the most wonderful
Sentence in your vocabulary:
"Here I am,
I'm listening."
And every time,
Every single time,

You touch, sniff, hear, feel, and notice,
You say to me,
"Here I am."
You will hear deeply.
You'll notice me
Walking,
Talking,
Calling you
Always
Into life.

NOTE TO SELF
Today, listen with all my senses to God's presence.

MAY 15

SARAH'S OFFERING

"Take your son, your only son, whom you love."
—Genesis 22:2

After all these years, was it really true? Sarah would have a son, whose name would redeem her own small faith and reduced view of God. His name would mean laughter, and with that one word Sarah's past would be healed, her reputation redeemed, and her mouth and heart filled with laughter and joy.

But wait. What's this? Her husband hauled out of bed, mumbling to their God. She followed him, pulling on his elbow. Trying to hear.

He was going to do *what*? Take their son, Isaac, to the mountain? Their only son, born of their life and love, born of their faith, born to redeem their old age and the madness of their nomadic life?

"No!" her heart screamed. It echoed off the cavern once filled with laughter. "No!" she shouted to him, pulling Abraham backward, trying to stop him.

And then she knew. She saw it all so clearly and rolled her lips inward to hold back the sobs. She wanted to yell and accuse this humble, irritating, gracious, risk-taking man, who'd thrown her to the wolves like last-night's leftovers more than once. "You don't love Isaac! You've always only loved Ishmael, and now that God ran him off, you don't want Isaac." Oh, she could go on and on about that. "He is *my* son, my only son. You will not do this." She grabbed his arms and threw herself in front of him to block his exit.

"Sarah." How dare he look at her with those sad eyes, those eyes full of both love and of loss? He said her name again. "Sarah." She watched tears form in the corners of his eyes. "I love you. I love our son. Just like you do." He waited, then shook an arm free to wipe away a tear. "But do we love our son more than we love God?"

Her heart rattled and died inside her rib cage. She swallowed, choking on her fury and pain. And on the truth. But how could she not love her son, whom she could see, more than the God she could not see?

Her bones shook. She released her grip on Abraham and pressed her hand to her chest. She buried her face in the folds of her robe. Her answer scraped out like a flint knife on a rock. "Yes."

Abraham reached for her chin and lifted it. "Yes." He swallowed, the pulse in his temple throbbing with emotion. "And we must offer this child back to God. Surely God will return him to us. For this God is the God of resurrection, of life. Hasn't God given life to our loins, that we might bring this life into the world?"

Sarah's breath lurched out and in. She nodded, the smallest, barest nod to the God who had called them. The God who had promised.

If God asked for their son, God knew the truth. She loved Isaac, laughing Isaac, more than God. She fell to her knees as Abraham left.

This was, perhaps, the one gift she had left to give. Her child, and thus her heart, back to God.

She crumpled on the floor of their tent.

And prayed for resurrection.

TRAVELING MERCY
Dear one,
Life has cost you so much,
But I am the one who loves you.
I will never ask you
For what I would not give you myself.
And one day
You will see
That I am in fact
Both the Resurrection
And the Life.
You will see.
In three days.
And I see
Your heart.
And where there are tears now
There will again be laughter.
I am the God who sees,
And you will see.
Three days, my love.

NOTE TO SELF
Look for resurrection pulse in the dying moments of today.

MAY 16

THE THORNS OF A DILEMMA

"The fire and the wood are here," Isaac said,
"but where is the lamb for the burnt offering?"

—Genesis 22:7

Isaac, jostled awake from a deep sleep, trundled out the door into the cold dawn air. When he could focus around his yawns, he saw the servants huddling in the semi-dark, and his father, eyes as big as dark grapes.

What could Isaac possibly think, when his father pulled him from his warm bed and they headed out through the wilderness with the servants tagging along? This was no father-son campout. No Boy Scout wilderness adventure.

His father chopped the wood—pretty impressive for a man his age, though why he didn't let the servants do it Isaac couldn't understand. He couldn't know what he didn't know: that some responsibilities were too personal to delegate. His father loaded the wood onto Isaac's shoulders. Because we know the story, the irony and almost cruelty of this single action hurts. Abraham put the wood for the burnt offering on Isaac's shoulders, the young man who would *be* the burnt offering unless God intervened. Wait. Isaac carried the wood for the fire that would kill him?

What did Isaac think? He noticed that they had the wood, the fire, and the knife. But something was missing. His first recorded word in Scripture is, "Father?"

"Yes, my son?"

"The fire and the wood are here. But where is the lamb for the burnt offering?"

"God himself will provide the lamb for the burnt offering, my son" (see Gen. 22:7–8). His father's answer should have consoled him. But we know the storyline. Any relief was temporary, a topical salve for this son, because at the top of the mountain, his father, his beloved father, built an altar and arranged the wood and then asked Isaac to lie on top, lashing him down.

And then Isaac knew the truth. He was the offering. The soon-to-be burnt offering. How could he be the lamb his father talked about?

He'd heard of this a time or two, of course, on the hush-hush. Heard of some religious fanatics in the surrounding countryside who threw babies into the fire. Child sacrifices to the gods to appease them or win some sort of favor. But his parents loved him. Their God was different, the almighty God, the great God. Such a thing would never happen. It hadn't crossed his mind to consider such an atrocity.

Isaac could have easily overpowered his aged father. He could have run away from the altar area. But he didn't. Somehow, in spite of this, he trusted his father. He held his breath, but couldn't shut his eyes as his father lifted the knife.

And then God intervened, halting the knife just a fraction of space from Isaac's throat. Isaac's heart started beating again, after it almost had burst in fear.

Sometimes, he thought, something changed in him from that point on.[1] Whatever his age, that day near Moriah, he was an abused child. His father had taken a knife to his throat and tied him up to set him on fire. It was the stuff of sensational journalism. In a future world, they arrested people for that, took their kids away from them. How would he ever trust his father again? Even more, how could he trust the God who said, "Sacrifice your son, your only son, on an altar"?

But on his better days, he remembered his father's words, his father's faith: "God will provide a lamb for the offering." He remembered, always with a catch of his own breath, the ram caught in the thorns.

And he couldn't possibly have known, then, that God intended all along to save him. That God would institute the redemption of the first-born of Israel through Isaac's very own great-grandchildren. And that, many years later, God would provide the first-born son, the Lamb, who would wear a crown plaited from thorns.

TRAVELING MERCY
Dear one,
Your pain is my own,
And believe me,
I understand.
But do not let your questions
Stop you from coming to me,
From inviting me in
To your life,
To your days,
To your questions,
To your hope.

I will provide.
I will always love you.
For you are my
Beloved child.

NOTE TO SELF
Just because I don't understand God's ways doesn't mean they're optional or I can walk away.

NOTE
1. Don't miss the follow-up deeper devotion book by Jane Rubietta, *Finding Your Name* (WPH), available 2015, as we journey with Isaac and then Jacob further into the life of faith.

MAY 17

THE SEE-TO-IT GOD

"Take your son, your only son, whom you love."
—Genesis 22:2

It's enough to make you wish you hadn't picked up the phone or tuned into the dream. Too bad you hadn't just buried your head in the pillow. To get an impossible order like that? Is God crazy, or is Abraham?

And isn't this what people say they fear, that if they answer God's call with, "Here I am," God will, in fact, require something drastic. It's a primary excuse for avoiding God's pressing on our souls. Because God will maybe, say, send you to the outer reaches of the known world where you not only wouldn't have power, food, or even water for that matter, running or not. You wouldn't even have cell-phone service and Wi-Fi. That God isn't of the dress-up-on-Sunday, blessing-giving God, but like the cruel designers of survival reality shows, dropping you off in nowhere-land surrounded by shark-infested waters and lions that roam about the jungle ready to devour you. And then God would ask you to swim for it and make converts along the way. That God would say, "Good luck," nod, and then, "You can do it. Use your head." That God delights in people's powerless plights.

Or just maybe, the deep, deep fear is that God would ask you to give up your loved ones to God's care.

Perhaps this is why we tiptoe around faith. We know that God asked Abraham to sacrifice his only son, Isaac, that long-awaited baby boy who was now about ready for his bar mitzvah or to step under the *chuppah* or to run one of the family enterprises, and who instead was given some rope and a stack of kindling and told to lie down on it.

We aren't sure we can trust that kind of God. So we hedge our faith a bit, smile a lot, nod, and memorize verses, but inside the jaws of our hearts clench as tight as bear traps. How do we trust the God who might ask for something so important?

There is an irresolvable tension between the God who tests—and the Scriptures are full of examples of God testing—and the God who provides. We do not want to be part of the testing side of God, and nearly two thousand years after Abraham, when Jesus said, "Pray like this, 'Lead us not into temptation,'" it's possible he referred to Abraham's testing.

Yet the God who tests is also always the God who provides. Listen! "No temptation has overtaken you except what is common to mankind. And God is faithful; he will not let you be tempted beyond what you can bear. But when you are tempted, he will also provide a way out so you can endure it" (1 Cor. 10:13). Here, the word *tempted* can also mean tested and testing. The testing need not win—God will always provide a way out.

We cannot remove the first part of the Abraham-God-Isaac triangle where God asks Abraham to sacrifice his son, his only son, from the second part of the story, the pivot point in the entire chapter: the place where God stops Abraham's hand.

God does not delight in sacrifice. He delights in obedience. God saw Abraham's faith, and he intervened. God provided. He literally "saw to it," in the Hebrew. He took care of it.

It is the same covenant. God takes care of heaven's side, and then God takes care of earth's side. The same God, the God who tests is the God who provides.

The God who loves.

TRAVELING MERCY
Dear one,
If I test you,
And that might be the case,
Then you can know
For absolute certainty
That I will also provide,
See to it,
Make a way out
Of the temptation.
So it is,
And so it has always been.
But now you have a Helper
Always on the ready.
This doesn't mean
I won't ask hard things,
Only that if I do
You will have the means
To get through them.

Because I am always
The God who sees,
The God who provides,
The God who loves.

NOTE TO SELF
Test time equals trust time equals God-always-provides time.

MAY 18

LEFT BEHIND

> Then Abraham returned to his servants, and they set
> off together for Beersheba.
>
> —GENESIS 22:19

Is it too much to ask, "What did Isaac do after that?" Why doesn't the record tell us that Abraham descended from the altar with Isaac holding onto his arm, helping his ancient father pick his way down the game trail? That they watched the flames engulf the wood and offering, with their arms about one another, rejoicing in heart and song at God's provision for a sacrificial animal? Or did Abraham leave Isaac up there, in that sacrificial area? His beloved son, whether thirteen or twenty-three or thirty-three, abandoned on the mountain?

Perhaps we don't know how Isaac returned because he has to get himself off the mountain—literally, yes, but also emotionally and spiritually. The mountain surely represents a turning point in his emotional and spiritual life, as well as in his relationship with his father.

After all, it's not every day that God asks you to sacrifice your child and you decide to do just that, much to everyone's stunned and traumatized amazement and horror, and then the order is rescinded one tick before the knife nicks the flesh.

Although, maybe it *is* every day. Doesn't God ask us, every single day of our lives, "How much do you love the people in your life? How much do you love the stuff in your life? The positions in your life? Have they become gods to you? And how much do you love me?"

And isn't it true that we have all felt like we were Isaac, sacrificed by another's priorities? Or wounded in spite of or even because of their attempts at faithfulness?

If you and I are Isaac, then we have to wrestle with the issues of abandonment that he surely experienced on the mountain. We have to battle the demons that suggest that God doesn't really love us, and here's the proof (imagine a long list, for surely it would be extensive). Life, just real life in a broken world with broken people, suggests that others put us somewhere down on the value scale, that we aren't up to bat first on the team, we aren't the MVP after all.

We can point to the people who dragged us up the mountain to sacrifice us, for we have all been there in one way or another (as have they). We can shake our fist at their God and our God, and turn our backs on such a God who would make such demands. We can refuse relationship with the people who hurt us, God, of course, included on that list. Anger could fuel the rest of our lives, and we could carry it like a flint box every step, always ready to set fire to the tinder and kindling around us.

But that will not bring us healing. That will not bring us to a place of wholeness. That will never set our foot on a path to freedom. Blame rarely results in bounty. Only barrenness.

So today, how about we revisit that mountain, or those mountains, and the people who took us there and even left us there, and the wounds that result. There we recognize our blame game and how it stunts us. And then we begin to bring those reactions to God.

Because God is the one who said, "I desire obedience and not sacrifice." God is the one who said, "A broken and contrite heart I will not despise" (see Ps. 51:17).

And we begin to climb down from the barren mountaintop of blame, and into bounty.

TRAVELING MERCY
Dear one,
Whether you are Isaac or Abraham
Or both,
You are my beloved child.
And you are the child
In whom I delight.
You are the one I called,
You are the one
In whom I have left
My promises.
Come down from the mountain
With me.
I will be your God,
And you will always be my child.
Do not let blame
Rob you of the bounty
Of my love.

NOTE TO SELF
Get out of the fire and get on with faith.

MAY 19

SHE (FINALLY) GETS HER OWN HEADER

Sarah lived to be a hundred and twenty-seven years old.
—Genesis 23:1

We have watched Sarah from a distance in these chapters in Genesis. She is rarely addressed directly and never consulted for wisdom or advice. With almost no spoken lines, she remains a nearly silent but principal character in the history of the Hebrew people. The headers in Scripture, up until chapter 23, concern others' adventures. In Genesis 23, Sarah finally merits her own header: "The Death of Sarah."

That's it. An obituary, not an adventure. Though not even an obituary, not in the traditional sense of reciting some lineage, survivors, and some significant life accomplishments.

Her tombstone might read: "Sarah. Wife of Abraham. Mother of Isaac. 127 years old. May she rest in peace."

We don't know her birthday or her mother's name. We don't know what century she died, let alone what year, only where: near Hebron in the land of Canaan. Some questions about her life remain unanswered. Like, why did Abraham, for instance, go to Hebron to mourn for her? Were they living separately? The text places him in Beersheba prior to this, after the return from Moriah in Genesis 22:19. We know this: She lived a life that allowed Abraham to mourn and grieve her passing, and that her only son, Isaac, grieved his mother's death until he married Rebekah.

Though Sarah is rarely referenced by name outside the book of Genesis, many years after her death God called Israel back by saying, "Look to the rock from which you were cut and to the quarry from which you were hewn; look to Abraham, your father, and to Sarah, who gave you birth" (Isa. 51:1–2). And we see, not the frustrated life of a woman thrown into the clutches of powerful rulers because of her husband's fear, not the bitter laugh of a barren woman who sent a slave and child off into the desert, but a woman whose life curved upward, like a grimace becoming a smile becoming a laugh. She did not live mired in negative memories that cemented into a bitter spirit. She lived victoriously in difficult places and grew strong like lilies of the valley, though she never lived to see God's promise fulfilled: "I will bless her so that she will be the mother of nations; kings of people will come from her" (Gen. 17:16).

A woman of legendary beauty, but more than that, of character. Bounty characterized her life, not barrenness, the amazing bounty of God's blessings over her and through her into the whole world. She, though once dead in the womb (Rom. 4:19), became alive with God's promises.

And isn't it so with us? In spite of our disappointments, in spite of barren places, God has given us life. God calls us out of barrenness into blessing, into everything we need to live well and to love well, into God's blessing over us and in us and through us into this world. God changed Sarah's bitterness into blessing after blessing and offers this conversion to us, this mysterious morphing from broken to rebuilt.

Man or woman, married or single, fulfilled or unfulfilled, our God calls us, just like Sarah, and promises us, just like Sarah. God invites us to step into the mystery, into a life bigger than we can imagine and a promise as unending as the grains of sand in the desert or stars in the sky.

TRAVELING MERCY
Dear one,
More than the grains of sand in the desert,
More than the stars in the sky.
You cannot number
My love for you,
Nor count on your fingers
My blessings over you
And through you.
Choose today
To live in bounty
Not barrenness,
And the world will be blessed
Through you.
Through us.
And we'll write the header
That says,
"We Lived."

NOTE TO SELF
Live in today's blessings not yesterday's bitterness.

MAY 20

REPUTATION IS EVERYTHING

> Abraham went to mourn for Sarah and to weep over her.
> —Genesis 23:2

Abraham mourned. He wept over Sarah at her death, weeping all the tears he had. He grieved, which is not something we are particularly good at doing, and not a process we honor in our get-over-it and get-on-with-it lives. He did the grief work necessary, but he didn't stay in his grief. When the proper time came for burial, he rose from her side, left her tent, and sought a burial spot.

In those days, cemeteries didn't try to sell you plots, rather, death happened and then you had a family burial site where you got your own shelf for your body until your bones went into a bone jar. Or because you were a new family in a new place, such as Abraham and Sarah, you sought out a site with a shelf and brought your own bone jar.

Abraham picked a spot near Mamre, near one of their first stops on the journey from Harran. There, after parting ways with Lot, Abraham had pitched his tent and built an altar to the Lord.

At Mamre, Abraham experienced God's presence and began to live into God's promises more fully. Decades later, again at Mamre, life came full circle with Sarah's death. Problem was, Abraham didn't own any land. Not a single blade of grass, not at Mamre or anywhere in the Promised Land.

But this spot came with a history. In spite of all his victorious forays and fame, he went in humility to buy it. "I am a foreigner and stranger among you." A resident alien, a settler, "only an outsider here," *The Message* says. Abraham undermined his status, mindful that, in fact, he had none, knowing he had no right to own land as a foreigner.

"You're a prince of God!" they protested (see Gen. 23:6 MSG). Take the field, take the cave that is in the field. I'll give it to you.

Abraham didn't want a gift, and he didn't want a bargain. He hadn't fought about the land when he moved there after Lot moved on, and he wasn't going to fight about it now. He expected to pay full price and refused their offer of a gift or a discount. He didn't presume upon his reputation as a prince in their eyes. Death is the great equalizer. We all pay full price.

When death knocked on his door, he answered with integrity. When he died, he, too, would join Sarah's bones in the family burial grounds. And when his son Isaac died, there he would be buried.

Fair and square, the family would have a burial place. But more than that, they would have a reputation to live up to. A reminder, before you go on that shelf, to live the life you want on the epitaph, first.

TRAVELING MERCY
Dear one,
You too are a foreigner
And stranger
In the land.
But not really,
Because you are mine
And I walk along beside you.
And the best way to prepare
For dying
Is to live with me now.
Then you'll be ready
No matter what.
But don't let anyone
Put you on the shelf
Too soon.

NOTE TO SELF
Die to tomorrow. Live well today.

MAY 21

LEADING THE WAY

"He will send his angel before you."

—Genesis 24:7

The longest chapter in the book of Genesis, chapter 24, details the faith of an anonymous servant[1] in carrying forward the promise of progeny to Abraham: "I will make you exceedingly, exceedingly numerous" and "exceedingly, exceedingly fruitful" (literal reading of Gen. 17:2, 6). If Isaac didn't get a wife, and the right one at that, nothing exceedingly, exceedingly would happen at all.

So when Abraham was "old *and* advanced in years" (Gen. 24:1 in the original language), he sent off his oldest servant to see about getting Isaac a wife to carry on the promise. This must have grieved Abraham, because one didn't send a servant to select a child's wife. But not just any wife: by now, Abraham knew that his brother had a passel of children and grandchildren (Gen. 22:20–23), and surely one of them would be suitable. Under no circumstances, however, was the wife to come from the Canaanites. To seal the command, Abraham promised that God "will send his angel before you so that you can get a wife for my son from there."

The servant asked Abraham good questions—which shows us just how trusted he was, as well as how skilled he was at his job—and headed off. If he came back empty-handed, he was not to bring Isaac back to the past, to the place of Abraham's younger days. That was behind him, and all of them.

This trusted man loaded up ten camels with an abundance of rich gifts and plodded off to the town of Nahor. When he arrived, he led his camels to the well outside of town.

He prayed. Not just, "God bless this trip." There was to be no guesswork about the girl. He prayed specifically, at length, about how God could highlight the right woman for the master's son. Of all the women who would come at sundown to draw water from the well, the only one to approach the servant should be the one chosen for Isaac. Not only that, but the servant had a script she needed to follow, as well.

And wonder of wonders, a gorgeous woman approached him and offered him water. And water for the camels as well.

This seems like simple enough common courtesy. But if the camels were empty, they could each need up to twenty-five gallons of water. Her jar held perhaps five or six. That's a lot of trips from the watering hole with a heavy jar (try carrying five gallons on your shoulder for a while).

The servant watched, his heart in his throat and his eyeballs twitching at this unfolding miracle. When he learned who she was—"I am the daughter of Bethuel, the son that Milkah bore to Nahor"—amazing! The very child of Abraham's brother (or brother's granddaughter, as some believe)! The final requirement, an offer of overnight hospitality, was fulfilled, and the man was overcome with joy.

He bowed down, right then and there, in front of the watering hole, in front of God and everybody, and worshiped the Lord.

The family all agreed to the marriage—which also seems miraculous—but tried to persuade him to stay ten times longer than the overnight.

This servant stuck to his guns, faithful to the last detail, the fiancée agreed, and the next day, they journeyed back to Abraham with a bride for Isaac.

The line would continue. The next generation of the "exceedingly, exceedingly" numerous multitude started right up when Isaac came in from the field and saw the woman who would be his wife, the woman of his dreams, his parents' dreams. God's dreams.

The servant? He shows us that anonymity does not equal insignificance. That God delights to answer specific prayers and reward obedience. And worship, well, worship is the best response ever to the work of God.

TRAVELING MERCY

Dear one,
My promise hasn't changed,
And I will still prepare the way for you.
I can send my angels ahead of you,
Lead you in the way you should go.
Don't hesitate to ask specifically,
To pray deeply,
And to worship greatly
When you see my hand.
And don't worry about fame
And if no one

Knows your name.
I do,
And have called you by name
And you are mine.
Exceedingly, exceedingly.
And gladly, gladly.

NOTE TO SELF
Be exceedingly, exceedingly grateful.

NOTE
1. Tradition suggests this might have been Eliezer (Gen. 15:2), but there is no certainty.

MAY 22

THE LIFE AND TIMES

Abraham lived a hundred and seventy-five years.

—Genesis 25:7

Someone living a 175 years, in our generation, would have seen not only World Wars I and II, but the Civil War and the Civil Rights movement. Would know life without electricity or even inside running water, have experienced the years pre-health insurance, and have seen Korea and the Cold War and Vietnam. Their lives would have included the assassination of both President Kennedy *and* President Lincoln. Electric typewriters and computers in your pocket. Men on the moon and rovers on Mars. Would have seen Vincent Van Gogh's *Starry Night* and heard the pop song of the same title in 1971. The first car and the first airplane, the first radio and silent movie, the first talkie and the first TV. Life and death. Unspeakable trauma and tragedy in massacres and bombings, military coups and political might.

It's a long time to live, and a lot of life to observe and participate in throughout those decades, to wonder if the world is a downhill luge run, an uphill battle, or both.

And how many times, through those 175 years, might we have been tempted to quit? Or even during our own more limited years, for that matter, likely half of Abraham's lifespan. To imagine that our presence doesn't matter or that our promises never come to fruition. To give up on God, to get a divorce from the One who made all those promises.

Rather than call it quits, what if we look backward so we can look forward again? So we can notice the surprising blessings and graces of our lives, and look at events as though pages in our scrapbook or the family photo album.

Such a journey would open us to the past presence of God and take away our fear of the future, our fear that we have dwindled away our lives and they count for nothing.

To review leads us through the answered and unanswered prayers of today, and the extended and extensive promises of tomorrow, heard, offered, but not yet received. How else do we circumvent doubt except to focus on the blessings, but more than that, on the God who blesses?

We might be flabbergasted to see God in many more moments than we realized. God, the ultimate photobomber.

Like Forrest Gump who managed to be in every key moment in history during his adult years, showing up in all the big pictures. Except that in this review of our lives, we would see God in not just the trophy shots, but also in the mundane minutes when we think no one is watching and no one cares and no one loves. Least of all us.

But to watch for God's presence in the moments of our lives is like watching a slow-developing Polaroid. It takes time to see the God-shot.

Imagine, though, if we could look at our lives and see the pictures of God, there in the ER, wedding chapel, funeral home, birthing room, pink-slip room, and unemployment line. See God in the back-alley moments and the center-stage seconds.

To see and fall for God all over again. Like the woman, determined to divorce her no-count husband, who started ripping out his pictures from their albums. But when she stopped to look at those snapshots, to remember the moments together, the events shared, and the person she'd married, she fell in love again. Their marriage thrives today after a near shipwreck on the rocks of discouragement and disappointment.

Whether 175 years or seventeen or seventy-five, when the going gets tough, go backward. Invite God to open your eyes to the supernatural presence of the God who promises, the God who blesses. The God who is the "I am" of all our yesterdays, tomorrows, and todays.

TRAVELING MERCY
Dear one,
I was there,
I am there,
I will always be there
For you.
But we must wait together
For the film of your life
To develop,
So you can see
Not only me,
But also yourself
As I see you,
And your life,
How it has carved a path
Through the mountains

Of this world
And created a highway
For people's blessings.
I have blessed you
And through you,
You will be a blessing
Always.
Because I am with you
Always.

NOTE TO SELF
I'm not. I can't.
You can. You're the I AM.

MAY 23

FULL OF YEARS

> Then Abraham breathed his last and died at a good
> old age, an old man and full of years.
>
> —Genesis 25:8

One hundred and seventy-five. "These are the days of the years of the lifetime of Abraham that he lived," the Hebrew reads. Old, absolutely. Full of years? Well, that's a choice, isn't it?

Abraham had a tremendous run at life, twice as long as anyone in our generation expects to live with any degree of health and vitality. Only a few people in Scripture receive the description after their name "old, and full of years." Isaac. King David. Jehoida. Job. That's about it. Evidently it was a challenge to be both at the same time.

Although genealogical tradition in those days ascribes the lengthier obituary to a person of prominence, it is still a challenge to be full of years. Old might or might not be a challenge. Some people have astounding longevity in their family line or wonderful health that makes it easier to grow old well or at least to grow old.

But to also live "full of years" is entirely another possibility.

Old may be inevitable. Full of years is optional. It's not too late for your obit to read that way.

Full of years, a daily regimen. Begin to live full, minute by minute and day by day until they add up to a pile of calendars jammed with, not a bunch of activities and scribbles in the little boxes, but life. Life, spilling out of the pores. Imagine, fullness as it describes our adventures, our hopes and dreams, the work God did in us and through us. Full of years, full of life, of joy, of thanksgiving. Full of years, regardless of whether our dreams come true or the promises we've been scanning the horizon for are fulfilled. Full of years, full of laughter and loving, full of tasting every morsel life offers (and I don't mean food, or you will just be full and then you might die and thus you also wouldn't be old). Full of years of living out the love God pours into you, full.

Full of years of listening to others' words, to their hearts, to their pain, to their flat-out happy feelings. Full of years of listening to God, to the Scriptures, to the gentle nudges and the full court press of the Holy Spirit. Full of marching forward into the hope that lies before you. Full of perseverance. Full, absolutely stuffed to the brim after a lifetime of tasting and seeing that the Lord is indeed good, better than good, the absolute best. Full.

Full, overflowing, exceedingly blessed to be a blessing. Exceedingly fruitful—love, joy, peace, patience, kindness, goodness, faithfulness, gentleness, self-control, and the list goes on and on.

What would it require? Breaking with your past. Breaking with your future. Living, really living, in today. In God's presence. With God's help.

Full. And tomorrow, we start over again.

Full. Of the days, of the years, of the lifetime that we live.

TRAVELING MERCY

Dear one,
Grace upon grace
Is how we get
To the place
Of old and full of years.
Because every day
We start over,
You and I,
And wipe clean the slate
Of yesterday's mistakes
And write a new life
Every day.
Yesterday? Tomorrow?
Just take today.
Tomorrow will take care of itself.
Exceedingly, exceedingly,
All the days of the years of the lifetime
That we live together.

NOTE TO SELF
Live full. Taste, see, and live fully today.

MAY 24

FRIEND OF GOD

> "Abraham believed God and it was credited to him as righteousness," and he was called God's friend.
>
> —JAMES 2:23

What better title could we imagine than being called "friend of God"? For this is how the Scriptures refer to Abraham: the friend of God. Friend of God! Consider this: Is there any higher honor, anything more humbling, knowing what we do of human nature and how far from perfect we all are? Freeze frames from Abraham's life show an imperfect human being, often afraid, sometimes succumbing to the temptation to fulfill God's promise through human means. And we see some of the fallout from his life choices: the diseases in Pharaoh's household, the barrenness in the king's, the difficulty in Hagar's family line that continues even to this day.

Even though we glimpse only snippets of Abraham's life, we see enough to know that we aren't dealing with a perfect man who behaved perfectly and thus earned the right to be called God's friend. What are we missing here?

One of the meanings for the word *friend* in Hebrew is "covenantal partner." And Abraham was God's covenantal partner, not because Abraham had anything to bring to the table, but because God cut the deal and then fulfilled the deal. Abraham believed that God could set him right (the meaning of righteousness) and was declared righteous before God.

The covenant. The loyalty. The friendship. A friendship based not on Abraham's perfection or his excellent character qualities; not on his victories in the battle of the kings or his rescue of Lot or on any other fine action on his part; and certainly not on his net worth and how much of his annual income he donated to the charities that constantly came calling for donations.

A friendship based on God saying yes to Abraham and Abraham saying yes to God. But Abraham was to live faithfully before God, to keep redirecting his gaze to the God who called, the God who covenanted. Abraham believed God, we're told in Genesis 15:6, and it was credited to him as righteousness.

James 2:22–23 clarifies how this looked as Abraham lived out that friendship with God: "You see that his faith and his actions were working together, and his faith was made complete by what he did. And the scripture was fulfilled that says, 'Abraham believed God, and it was credited to him as righteousness,' and he was called God's friend." But back up a moment: James 2:21 gets a running start into the discussion about righteousness and friendship with God by reminding us that Abraham offered up his son Isaac on the altar. Was he righteous because he wanted to kill his son?

No. Righteous, because he fully trusted God and responded in obedience. He tried to live out that righteousness.

God said yes and made a huge promise to Abraham. Abraham said yes and made a promise to God. Then they both lived up to their promise—God perfectly, Abraham imperfectly.

And because of God's perfection, we call imperfect Abraham who said yes, a friend of God.

TRAVELING MERCY
Dear one,
I'm not looking
For a few good men and women.
There aren't any,
Not by my standards.
I'm looking for someone
To call my friend.
Someone who believes
That in me
They are set right,
In me
They are put right,
In me
They have an eternal partnership.
That's it.
So put aside your not-rights
And your not-set-rights
And say yes to me.
It's a yes
That will last
For all eternity.
What do you say to that?
Hopefully, yes.

NOTE TO SELF
Live in God's yes. Look to bless.

MAY 25

LIVING LIKE A FRIEND

"Father Abraham, have pity on me."
—Luke 16:24

Abraham lived into the name "friend." He championed the cause of any righteous person in Sodom and Gomorrah, should God find any, including Lot. Abraham stood in the gap for his first-born son, the son of the slave-woman Hagar, when he cried out to God, "Oh, if only Ishmael might live before you!"

So when we jump to the New Testament, we shouldn't be surprised at Jesus' story about Abraham, a rich man, and a poor man (see Luke 16:19–31).

Seems a poor beggar named Lazarus, covered with sores, lay starving and dying on a rich man's stoop. He only wanted a few crumbs from the rich man's groaning banquet table. The rich man told him to shape up and go get a job, the world was going to pot because of people like him, and why was he dirtying up his doorstep anyway? He should just pull himself up by his bootstraps and start getting himself together.

Soon the angels came and took away Lazarus to Abraham's side. Before long, the rich man also died and was buried. In hell, thirsty as a man floating on the Dead Sea, he looked up and saw Abraham so far away in heaven. He squinted through the heat waves, and there was that disgusting beggar right at Abraham's side!

But notice how cool and comfortable the beggar looked up there next to Abraham, his skin now smooth and young, his sores healed. "Father Abraham," the rich man begged (see who's begging now?). "Just send Lazarus down to drip a little cold water from his finger into my mouth. My tongue is melting in this inferno."

"Son," Abraham answered (the word may be an affectionate term, as in "my child," which reminds us that Abraham did not judge but acted with kindness and lived into the role and name of a good father), "Lazarus got nothing on earth, and you got everything. Now the situations are reversed, and now there's no way across that great divide."

"Son," he said to the rich man. Child, he called him. He didn't call him spoiled or selfish or mean-hearted. He didn't say, "You were an ugly lout dressed in fine purple, a pig in a silk robe." He called him son, child. He welcomed Lazarus the beggar, covered with sores, and he kindly answered the rich man, who'd already had his reward.

Unlike our record of Abraham, the rich man lived indifferent to the plight of the poor, the disadvantaged, the needy, and the marginalized. Because, after all is said and done, God sees the heart, and God watches to see how the heart is lived out in one's life. Nehemiah said to God about Abraham, "You found his heart faithful to you" (Neh. 9:8).

May it be so for us, as well.

TRAVELING MERCY

Dear one,
Child,
Son,
Daughter,
How I long
To welcome you
To my side
And to watch you
Welcome others
To your side.
May I find your heart
Faithful.
As you trust in me
You will be
Faithful.

NOTE TO SELF
Live today for a no-regret tomorrow.

MAY 26

SON OF ABRAHAM

> "Today salvation has come to this house,
> because this man, too, is a son of Abraham."
>
> —LUKE 19:9

Many years after Isaac, "son of Abraham," was born, another man's history would read, "This is the genealogy of Jesus the Messiah the son of David, the son of Abraham . . ." (Matt. 1:1).

The son of Abraham! This man would turn religion upside down, pulling the title of "righteous" away from the religious elite and giving it to people who, like Abraham, believed God and were therefore credited with righteousness. Not because they observed all the details of the law, but because they were put right by God. Jesus, baptized in the Jordan River, said, "It is proper to . . . fulfill all righteousness" (Matt. 3:15) and thereby angered anyone trying to fulfill the bill by legal means.

This Jesus would shout out, "Follow me!" to filthy fishermen and prostitutes, women caught in adultery and common thieves, people unlearned and people born with silver spoons in their mouths. He would dine with tax collectors and call priests hypocrites. He didn't care what people thought of him but wanted them to know what he thought of them: he loved them. He wanted them to live in that love, to live out of that love.

So one day, Jesus told a story about a Pharisee who stood apart from everyone else at the temple and looked down his self-righteous nose. He made a spectacle of praying big important prayers and thankfulness that he wasn't like anyone else—all the robbers, evildoers, and adulterers.

Meanwhile, a second man stood at a distance, too filled with remorse to even glance at the heavens. Head lowered, he beat his chest in anguish and prayed, "God, have mercy on me, a sinner." This man, Jesus said, went home justified (see Luke 18:13–14).

The crowds gathered and followed Jesus, this son of Abraham, with his revolutionary words and reconstruction of faith. One day, Jesus passed through Jericho and a living, breathing tax collector heard he was headed that way.

A tax collector named Zacchaeus, whose name meant "righteous one, pure one," wanted to see Jesus, and more than that, Jesus wanted to see him and followed him home for dinner. Zacchaeus cooked a feast of enormous proportions. The people, horrified that Jesus would eat with this little man with his huge list of sins, muttered and sniffed, "He has gone to be the guest of a sinner."

(Like Jesus had any other choices? He'd have eaten every meal alone for his entire life if he couldn't eat with sinners.)

But Zacchaeus lived into his name, emptying himself of sin and turning over his checkbook and Swiss bank account to heaven.

And Jesus? He called this man a son of Abraham. Son of Abraham!

Imagine the fury of the local self-righteous. Imagine Abraham's smile.

TRAVELING MERCY
Dear one,
You too are a child
Of Abraham
If you have said yes
To my only Son,
The son of Abraham.
And you are my child
As you live into your name,
"Righteous One,"
Not because of your own merits,
But because of my Son's
On your behalf.
Go ahead!
Empty your pockets
Of all your do-gooding
And all the wooden nickels
Of sin and self-righteousness,
And put it all
Into the offering basket.
Give it up,
Get over it,
Get on with it,
Child of Abraham.
Child of God.

NOTE TO SELF
Have a meal with Jesus, son of Abraham, and live into your name: child of God.

MAY 27

SOME FAMOUS AND NOT-SO-FAMOUS FRIENDS OF GOD

"I have called you friends."

—John 15:15

Who would you call a friend of God? When I consider that, I think of big names, like Albert Schweitzer or Mother Teresa. Hudson Taylor, Corrie ten Boom, or Archbishop Oscar Romero, the priest assassinated in 1980 for calling the army in San Salvador to act like Christians. Or to go back a couple of millennia: How about Peter or James or Paul, all martyred for the sake of God. Surely they were friends of God. John the Baptist, with his head on a platter for speaking the truth. Surely a friend of God.

I don't think of common, everyday people doing common, everyday things, people like me, being called a friend of God. I feel far from God's friend in practicality, though theologically it must be true. Acquaintance, yes. A sloppy servant, maybe. Relative, perhaps, but maybe the rebel of the family, the one with ADHD who can't remember what she started to say and so has terribly lopsided and muddled conversations with God and runs off on errands for God and forgets where she was going and ends up on a back road somewhere. But friend of God?

No, not so much. That's like saying I'm a friend of the president or a princess from another land and that I'm the go-to they call in the middle of the night when they are bored or lonely or troubled and need a listening ear. That when God is looking for someone to do something, he would call me. "Can you come early and help me set up for that banquet?" "Would you mind coming over to help me pack up the house and get it ready to sell?" Like I'm on God's speed-dial.

That's a friend, someone there in the hard times and the good times, the grieving and the laughter, the horrors and the honors. The set-up and the tear-down. Someone with sleeves rolled up and paint all over them. Someone ready to help unplug the sewer line or emcee the award ceremony. Willing to do the non-glory jobs and not worried about the glory jobs.

"Who will go for me?" God asked Isaiah. He replied, "Here am I. Send me."

Isn't that what God essentially asked Abraham? "Who will go for me? Who will speak for me? Who will be on my side?"

If that's the case, then every time we show up for the work of the kingdom, we say, "Here I am, send me." Every time we give someone a lift in the car or a lift of the spirits, we say, "Here I am, send me." Every time we wash a load of laundry or wash someone's feet, we say, "Here I am, send me." Every time we play pat-a-cake or pat a shoulder, we say, "Here I am, send me."

Maybe it's like grade school, and every time the teacher asks, "Who wants to clean the blackboard?" (or white board or smart board or . . .) we perch on the edge of our seats and raise our hand, saying, "Ooh, ooh, here I am. Send me." Empty the wastebasket? "Here I am." Visit the prisoner? "Here I am, send me." The hungry? The sick?

A friend of God? "Here I am, send me." Because why? A friend of God *acts* like a friend of God.

TRAVELING MERCY
Dear one,
See how it works?
I declare you my friend
And it is known that you
Are my friend,
And then you go
And act like my friend.
It's simple.
But it's not always easy.
But know this:
I'll never ask you to do
What I wouldn't do myself.
Just look at my Son,
If you wonder
How a friend looks.
Like him.
Like me.
Like you.

NOTE TO SELF
How will I act like God's friend today?

MAY 28

THE GREAT REVEAL

"You are my friends."

—JOHN 15:14

Abraham, friend of God. We're swimming in water way over our heads with this one, because we know we don't deserve that label. Check out these other uses of the same word, *friend*: 2 Chronicles 20:7; Proverbs 18:24; 27:6; and Isaiah 41:8. These verses show us how a friend lives, side by side on earth. The outworking of friendship.

Jump to the New Testament, to Jesus' words after a late night meal that signals, for us, the beginning of the end of his earthly ministry. Outside, the night sky an infinite arch overhead, stars too many to be counted. Inside, Jesus described how a friend looks.

"Greater love has no one than this: to lay down one's life for one's friends. You are my friends if you do what I command" (John 15:13–14). Being a friend looks like a willingness to take a hit, to go down for someone else. It looks like obedience to Jesus.

The water's over our heads again, and we just realized we can't swim. But wait. That's not the most startling use of the *friend* word. Because next, we hear the mind-boggling word used in an entirely new context, a heaven-come-to-earth context.

"I have called you friends," Jesus said. Friends! First he described what friends look like, how they live, then called the disciples friends. This, right *before* they abandoned him at the prayer vigil, *before* they skulked away once the guards arrest Jesus. *Before* they froze in fear after his death. *Before* they acted in obedience after his resurrection.

Jesus proclaimed these people, these very human, human beings, friends. And a friend sticks by another's side, no matter what, right?

Well, yes. Ideally. But they didn't. Not then. Eventually, they stuck closer and closer to Jesus. But it was a long obedience, a lifelong pursuit.

This is exactly how it goes. A lifelong, growing friendship. A covenantal partnership.

First, "You are my friends if you do what I command."

Second, "I have called you friends."

Next, here's what a friend looks like: someone who bears fruit (John 15:16). "I chose you and appointed you so that you might go and bear fruit—fruit that will last."

So go and do that, Jesus says. Live into your name. "My command is this: Love each other as I have loved you. . . . This is my command: Love each other" (John 15:12, 17). A friend looks like love, which looks like fruit, which looks like love.

Jesus says: I've called you friend and now I call it out in you: go and act like friends. Love people.

Not long after Jesus' death and resurrection, the disciples— his friends—jumped ship and headed back to their former fishing life. They fished all night and caught nothing. At dawn, a man on the shore said, "Friends, haven't you any fish?" (John 21:5). No fruit there.

They couldn't bear fruit on their own, couldn't catch fish without help. "Apart from me you can do nothing," Jesus had told them that night at dinner before he was crucified (John 15:5). So what did they do? What do we do?

We throw our nets into the water at his command and he brings the fish into the net and helps us drag the net to the shore. And then what? We lay the fish at his feet.

From barren nets to a bounty of fish. Fruit!

And what does bounty, fruit, look like, one more time? Like loving.

Jesus staked his life on that promise.

TRAVEL MERCIES
Dear one,
Do you see me
Smiling at you?
I've called you friend.
My Son declared you friend
And showed you what it looks like.
But he didn't stop there,
He sent the Friend,
The Comforter,
The Holy Spirit
To help you
Love.
So go ahead,
Wet the line;
Throw in your net.

And let's show the world
What a friend looks like.
It's time to love
Again.

NOTE TO SELF
Catch fish by loving others.

MAY 29

HOME SWEET HOME

By faith he made his home in the promised land
like a stranger in a foreign country.

—HEBREWS 11:9

Abraham uprooted his life and his wife and all his possessions, and trailed God around the continent for the rest of his 175 years. He heard, over and over again, that he was to inherit the Promised Land. He walked it, surveyed it, studied it, chased kings around on it, raised a family on it, and grazed his animals on it. He watched sunrises and sunsets. He saw seasons turn and crops ripen. But he never owned the land. No deed, no title. Nothing except a verbal promise and a child of that promise, Isaac.

At his time of death, the sole recorded land belonging to Abraham was his burial plot, a cave near his favorite trees of Mamre.

The Scriptures place him at Mamre several times. It is the spot of the third altar he built as a memorial to the Lord: "So Abram went to live near the great trees of Mamre at Hebron, where he pitched his tents. There he built an altar to the LORD" (Gen. 13:18). He loved that land and loved that spot of land. At Mamre he'd entertained the heavenly guests and begged for Lot's life and gotten the good word about Sarah's pregnancy. There, thirty-seven years later, he purchased the cave to bury his wife.

The only land Abraham owned was his burial plot. He died without ever reaching home.

Wait with that thought. Wait with that, the idea that you will never have your own front door with your name on it, that you will have no area code to call your own, no welcome mat, not really, not one that belongs to you.

Do you feel that hole in your chest, that cave of emptiness and longing that yearns for home?

Are you sad for this old man, whose faith never quit, and for his continual search for a home he never owned and never would own? For the man who would die and the only people who would visit his land would be those who added his son and grandsons' bones to the cave?

Even so, Abraham was not homeless, and his belongings at no time consisted of his possessions. He belonged to God. He kept his face fixed on God and knew himself to be a friend of God. He was never homeless. Because when you are loved, you have a home.

Maybe that's really what it means, that old saying: Home is where your heart is.

TRAVELING MERCY
Dear one,
You cannot
Be homeless
If you are loved.
And you are loved.

You are loved
Beyond all reason,
Beyond all merit.
And you will never be homeless.
But there are a lot of people
Wandering around
Without a home.
If you can love them
In my name
Then they too will know
What home means.
Home,
Sweet home.

NOTE TO SELF
If I'm always home in God's love,
then my life is a welcome sign to others.

MAY 30

CHILDREN OF THE PROMISE

It is the children of the promise who are regarded
as Abraham's offspring.

—ROMANS 9:8

The sun stains the horizon with orange, the color of an infant day lily. A perfectly clear day dawns, the last star still pinned to the sky and a moon shaving dangling from an invisible wire. The sun rises and swallows the night, and we rise and follow the God who promised.

The promise of a new day, a day to live into God's promises. To hitchhike with this God who called us from obscurity. To embrace this great gift of God blessing us in unique ways. The great promise—I will bless you and make your name great, and you will be a blessing; and I will take care of any who curse you—this promise rolls out through the generations.

Every day we live free; we live as children of the promise rather than slaves of the law, put right like Abraham, put right by Christ who fulfilled all righteousness. Every day we look at the God who calls us away from our enslavements into the reality of adoption with the full rights of the family of promise.

Every day we leave our Ur. Every day we live into the promise—seeing the God who blesses and recognizing those undeserved blessings. Every day we move from the barrenness of the past—regrets, mistakes, failures, tragedies, insufficiencies, bitterness—and head into the bounty of this astounding gift of blessing. We turn, like children with buckets filled to the brim with water, and the waters of blessing slosh over the sides of our lives into this world, a sweeping tide of blessing.

We welcome the visitors and bake the fresh bread of kindness and feed the warriors and water the camels. We stand in the gap, a go-between, and find our hearts changed by that turn of the blessing wheel.

Every day we invite God to convert the wounds from and in this world into the marks of people who follow the blessing, as we circumcise our hearts with the great truth of God's love and live into and out of that love.

We revisit the altars where we have seen God and heard God's promise, we stoke the fire of faith and remember that there are wheels on wagons for a reason, and we carry our flint box of warm encounters with God with us into this new day. God's presence warms us, and we in turn offer warmth to the cold hands of the disillusioned we meet along the path.

Child of the promise. Blessed to be a blessing. Free to live fully this day into the bounty of being loved and loving in return.

We find our promise when we look to God, and God converts our barrenness into bounty as we spill blessing into the world.

The nighttime of despair crashes on the rim of a new day, and we become part of the sunrise in this world, the light of God in us swallowing the darkness.

TRAVELING MERCY

Dear one,
The promise remains
Day after day after day.
And every single day
You wake up,
And I bless you,
And you bless others.
And with every blessing
The darkness diminishes
And the sun grows brighter.
You spill light over this world
And water the parched soils
Of disappointed people,
And the wilderness blooms
With my presence,
My promise,
My bounty.
Live, child of promise!
Live into the promise.
Live into the blessing.
Live out of the blessing.
Live out the blessing.
Because the sunrise from on high has come.
Open your hands
And open your heart
And open your mouth,
And the sun will pour out
Warm hope,
Spilling every single day.

NOTE TO SELF

Today the sun wins. God wins.
We win over the world with God's love.

MAY 31

PRESENT AND ACCOUNTED FOR

By faith Abraham . . .
—Hebrews 11:8

Abraham was not the only person called out of Ur, called to follow an unknown God out of his comfortable life with its inevitable difficulties and disappointments, perks and pleasures. Called to follow into an unknown land, to trust in promises he could not see, and to wait for many years to see those promises fulfilled, in part, at least, but never in full. And then called to give up everything promised, received or not, to demonstrate his love for God.

For isn't that your story, as well? To respond to the call of God, or what you suspect is the call of God, a God you have not known well or deeply or perhaps even at all, and to follow, not knowing where that God would lead you?

Called to trust in Someone you can't see, and called to keep trusting when the title and deed and offspring and promises aren't quite fulfilled. Called to break with your past, to absolutely walk away from all that would hold you back, good or bad, and then, like Abraham, to break with your future, your hope for the future, your imaginations about the future, your big plans for the future. To collapse all those, like a great hand of cards, and return them to the table. And then, with all that breaking and severing, called to live right now, today, trusting the God who makes the promises even when those promises tarry.

This is how the author of Hebrews, the book of crossing-over people, defined faith: "Now faith is confidence in what we hope for and assurance about what we do not see. This is what the ancients were commended for" (Heb. 11:1–2).

Yes, the ancients. Abel, Enoch, Noah, Abraham, Sarah, Isaac, Jacob, Joseph, Moses. And the roll call continues, clear to Christ Jesus, through centuries of people who trust God for the unseen. All the way to you. This is the biggest All Saints Day roll call to date.

And so the question is, when God calls roll today, how do we answer? Past? Future? Or present?

Here, God. Here I am.

And here, God, we say, as we empty all our pockets of our little gods, our personal and family and country gods— the gods of profit, or fame, or successful children, or big jobs, or bestsellers, or no-failures. As we throw down our small change worth nothing in the currency of faith.

And then, empty-handed, the lining of our soul's pockets hanging out, we answer again. Present. Here.

Isn't that the only way to live into the promise, to find the promise we've been waiting for all our lives? The elusive, around-the-next-corner hope for better.

We find, then, with our open hands, that we actually have everything we need. The promise of today, and the promise that the One who holds tomorrow will bring it to pass.

All in good time. God's time. And eventually, our watch will sync with God's, and we will live forever on God's clock. Eternity, gathered together, rolled into one.

How do we know? God promised.

Today. Present. Here I am.

TRAVELING MERCY
Dear one,
And here
I am
As well,
Delighted with you,
Delighted for today,
Delighted to unfurl
My promises
Day by day
And promise by promise
And hope by hope.
It's the only way to live.
Right now,
Present,
I am with you.
Today,
Always,
And forever.
Keep walking,
Keep watching,
Because hope lasts.
And one day
You will see.

NOTE TO SELF
What's in my pockets?

ABOUT THE AUTHOR

Jane Rubietta has a degree in marketing and management from Indiana University School of Business and attended Trinity Divinity School in Deerfield, Illinois.

Jane's hundreds of articles about soul care and restoration have appeared in many periodicals, including *Today's Christian Woman*, *Virtue*, *Marriage Partnership*, *Just Between Us*, *Conversations Journal*, *Decision*, *Christian Reader*, *Indeed*, and *Christianity Today*. Some of her books include: *Finding Life*, *Finding the Messiah*, *Quiet Places*, *Come Along*, *Come Closer*, *Grace Points*, *Resting Place*, and *How to Keep the Pastor You Love*.

She is a dynamic, vulnerable, humorous speaker at conferences, retreats, and pulpits around the world. Jane particularly loves offering respite and soul care to people in leadership. She has worked with Christian leaders and laity in Japan, Mexico, the Philippines, Guatemala, Europe, the US, and Canada.

Jane's husband, Rich, is a pastor, award-winning music producer, and itinerant worship leader. They have three children and make their home surrounded by slightly overwhelming gardening opportunities in the Midwest.

For more information about inviting Jane Rubietta to speak at a conference, retreat, or banquet, please contact her at:

Jane@JaneRubietta.com
www.JaneRubietta.com

From Eden to Gethsemane—
the Garden Restored

The life lost in Eden is found through Gethsemane. Follow author Jane Rubietta on her daily journey through the season of Lent as she traces the way that God the Son traverses with his people. Significantly, Jesus' ministry sometimes took place in garden settings: not only did he come because of what had been lost in Eden, but Jesus met with his disciples in a garden, he prayed in a garden, he was arrested violently in a garden, and he was buried in a garden tomb.

A free group leader's guide is available at www.wphresources.com/findinglife.

Finding Life
ISBN: 978-0-89827-892-7
eBook: 978-0-89827-893-4

1.800.493.7539   **W**   wphstore.com

From Darkness to Dawn—
the Birth of Our Savior

Through artfully told daily devotions, author Jane Rubietta leads readers along a twenty-eight day journey into the heart of Advent, in search of the living Messiah. Reaching past the holiday veneer of tradition, pageantry, and glitz, she draws readers far into the spiritual depths of Christmas, where Christ can be born again into souls. This deeper approach to devotion is still accessible reading for just five to ten minutes a day.

*A free group leader's guide is available at
www.wphresources.com/findingthemessiah.*

Finding the Messiah
ISBN: 978-0-89827-902-3
eBook: 978-0-89827-903-0

1.800.493.7539   wphstore.com

Finding Jesus in Every Season

Follow author Jane Rubietta on her daily journey through each season of the year to gain perspective, refresh your soul, and continue the journey. Tracing the lives of some of the Bible's greatest characters, these are transformational devotionals that encourage great depth. Walk through these stories from the Bible and experience life as these great characters did, gaining fresh faith and hope for your journey along the way.

A free group leader's guide will be available for each devotional at www.wphresources.com.

Finding Your Promise
(spring)
ISBN: 978-0-89827-896-5
eBook: 978-0-89827-897-2

Finding Your Name
(summer)
ISBN: 978-0-89827-898-9
eBook: 978-0-89827-899-6

Finding Your Dream
(fall)
ISBN: 978-0-89827-900-9
eBook: 978-0-89827-901-6

Finding Your Way
(winter)
ISBN: 978-0-89827-894-1
eBook: 978-0-89827-895-8

1.800.493.7539   wphstore.com